THE HAMLYN
THIRTY-SEVENTH SERIES

Law and Order

AUSTRALIA AND NEW ZEALAND
The Law Book Company Ltd.
Sydney: Melbourne: Perth

CANADA
The Carswell Company Ltd.
Agincourt, Ontario

INDIA
N. M. Tripathi Private Ltd.
Bombay
and
Eastern Law House Private Ltd.
Calcutta and Delhi
M.P.P. House
Bangalore

ISRAEL
Steimatzky's Agency Ltd.
Jerusalem: Tel Aviv: Haifa

MALAYSIA: SINGAPORE: BRUNEI
Malayan Law Journal (Pte.) Ltd.
Singapore

PAKISTAN
Pakistan Law House
Karachi

UNITED STATES
Westview Press
Boulder, Colorado

LAW AND ORDER

by

RALF DAHRENDORF, K.B.E., F.B.A.

*Professor of Social Science in the
University of Constance, formerly Director
of the London School of Economics*

Published under the auspices of

THE HAMLYN TRUST

LONDON
STEVENS & SONS
1985

Published in 1985
by Stevens & Sons Ltd.,
11 New Fetter Lane, London
Computerset by Promenade Graphics Ltd., Cheltenham
and printed in Great Britain by Page Bros. (Norwich) Ltd.

British Library Cataloguing in Publication Data

Dahrendorf, Ralf
    Law and order.—(Hamlyn lectures)
    1. Great Britain—Social conditions—1945–
    I. Title   II. Series
    941.085'8   HN385.5

    ISBN 0–420–47240–1
    ISBN 0–420–47250–9 Pbk

CONTENTS

THE HAMLYN LECTURES

THE HAMLYN TRUST

The Hamlyn Trust came into existence under the will of the late Miss Emma Warburton Hamlyn, of Torquay, who died in 1941 at the age of eighty. She came of an old and well-known Devon family. Her father, William Bussell Hamlyn, practised in Torquay as a solicitor for many years. She was a woman of strong character, intelligent and cultured, well versed in literature, music and art, and a lover of her country. She inherited a taste for law and studied the subject. She also travelled frequently to the Continent and about the Mediterranean, and gathered impressions of comparative jurisprudence and ethnology.

Miss Hamlyn bequeathed the residue of her estate in terms which were thought vague. The matter was taken to the Chancery Division of the High Court, which on November 29, 1948, approved a Scheme for the administration of the Trust. Paragraph 3 of the Scheme is as follows:

> "The object of the charity is the furtherance by lectures or otherwise among the Common People of the United Kingdom of Great Britain and Northern Ireland of the knowledge of the Comparative Jurisprudence and the Ethnology of the chief European countries including the United Kingdom, and the circumstances of the growth of such jurisprudence to the intent that the Common People of the United Kingdom may realise the privileges which in law and custom they enjoy in comparison with other European Peoples and realising and appreciating such privileges may recognise the responsibilities and obligations attaching to them."

FOREWORD

The title of this little book, *Law and Order*, sounds technical. It alludes to a problem of criminology, and also to a
plank in the platform of the political right. The argument
of the book however is not primarily technical. It takes the
terrors of our streets and the riots on our football grounds
as its point of departure, but then goes on to such issues as
the disorientation of the young, unemployment, and
cracks in the party system. In other words, this is a book
about social order and liberty.

As an unreconstructed eighteenth-century liberal, I
believe that big subjects must be treated in a lighter vein
than more limited ones. I was therefore pleased to be
invited to give the Hamlyn Lectures with their distinguished tradition, and their Scheme which emphasises
the "privileges" as well as the "responsibilities and obli-
gations" of "law and custom" especially in their English
version. While the book is almost twice as long as the lectures, I have kept their format, including the licence which
this art form permits to leave an argument suspended in
mid-air, change the subject, and raise questions without
giving definitive answers. In this sense, the little book is a
programme as much as a complete product, and indeed a
programme which contains no promise that it will ever be
completed by its author.

Easter 1985   R.D.

1. The Road to Anomia

In Berlin, at the end of April 1945, the signs of decomposition were unmistakable. I was not the only one in our quiet suburban street who had been hiding for weeks in a kind of voluntary house arrest. Next door, a young man who had been on the way to his army unit, had extended his visit to relatives indefinitely to await the end. Now, things were changing. Across the road, SS officers no longer went in and out of the home of the pretty widow and her two daughters; soon their bedsheets would be hung outside their windows to indicate surrender to officers of the occupation forces. Others were less adaptable. The retired military man a little further up the road was loading his gun in order to kill first his wife, then himself because the couple could not bear the moment of national shame. Elsewhere, shots were fired more arbitrarily. A young fanatic wounded a fellow Hitler Youth leader who had dared suggest that Hitler had led Germany into disaster. Was the *Führer* still alive? Suddenly, it became clear that there was no authority left, none at all.

Rumours started flying. The army stores in the nearby wood had been deserted! Could it be true? The young man next door and I went to see, found the stores without any sign of guards or occupants, grabbed a tray with some 50 pounds of fresh meat and carried it home where my mother proceeded to boil it in the washtub in the basement. The shops around the nearby subway station had been left by their owners! When I got there, dozens, perhaps hundreds of people were dismantling counters and shelves; what goods there had been, had already been taken. The only exception was the bookshop, where connoisseurs were selecting what they wanted. I still have the five slim volumes of romantic poetry which I acquired on that occasion. Acquired? Everyone carried bags and suitcases full of stolen things home. Stolen? Perhaps, taken is more correct, because even the word, stealing, seemed to have lost its meaning.

Then the first Russian officers walked up our street, reminding us that new authorities were not far. They began their rule as the old ones had finished theirs, with a splurge of arbitrary acts of violence, and very occasionally, of sympathy as well. When my history teacher, an anti-Nazi of Prussian convictions, opened the door of his house, he was simply shot dead by a Russian soldier. The elderly lady whom a soldier on horseback asked why she was crying, and who explained that another soldier had just taken her bicycle, stood bewildered when the Russian stepped down, handed her the reins and softly told her to take his horse instead. The war of all against all was also a state of spontaneous compassion. And of course, both did not last. The supreme, horrible moment of utter lawlessness was but a holding of breath between two regimes which were breathing equally heavily down the spines of their subjects. Like the fearful ecstasy of revolution, the moment passed. While yesterday's absolute law became tomorrow's absolute injustice—and yesterday's injustice tomorrow's law—there was a brief pause of anomy, a few days, no more, with a few weeks on either side first to disassemble, then to re-establish norms.[1]

These are lectures about law and order. I shall presently turn to the contemporary experiences to which this notion ordinarily refers, and throughout the argument, we shall not loose sight of the implications of an emphatic "law and order" attitude and policy. But to begin with Berlin—it might conceivably have been Beirut, or even Belfast—is more than an anecdotal whim. These lectures are not intended to be a technical contribution to criminology or the debate about prisons and the police. They are rather, a contribution to social and political analysis, and more precisely, to the analysis of social conflict and the political theory of liberalism.

Let me outline what I am planning to do, before I return to Berlin and to the facts about law and order. Traditional class struggles are no longer the dominant expression of the unsociable sociability of man. Instead, we find more individual and more occasional manifestations of social aggression. Violations of the law and breaches of public order by individuals, gangs and crowds are prominent among them. In the first lecture, we shall try to establish the facts and make sense of them so that the underlying social problem becomes apparent. The second and third lectures will be devoted to explanation, or more cautiously perhaps, to understanding the context. On the level of motives and ideas, the declining effectiveness of the law may be described as one of the contradictions of modernity by which we are surrounded wherever we look in the present world, from the Welfare State which actually creates a new poverty to the nuclear threat which reminds us daily of the ambivalence of human reason. We wanted a society of autonomous citizens, and we have created a society of frightened or aggressive human beings. We sought Rousseau, and we have found Hobbes. On the level of social and political forces, the new and as yet barely comprehended conflict is a result of the tendency, on the part of a large majority class, to define people out at the boundary in order to protect its own position. As a result, the dominant issue is not the redistribution of scarce resources within an accepted framework—unless one wants to describe membership of society itself as a scarce resource—but the social contract. Thus our thesis is that law and order present the major subject of conflict in the developed societies of the free world. That this should be so, is the seemingly paradoxical result of a century of applied enlightenment and expanding citizenship rights. The question remains what can be done about the new struggle for the social contract. The fourth lecture deals with solutions, or at any rate answers. Few such answers have been offered, and some are more frightening than the problem. There is a tendency for the arteries of the official society to harden and for those who have the power to respond with "law and order" measures in the common political sense. It can still be said that "the enemy"—the effective enemy of freedom that is—"stands on the right" (as the German Chancellor Wirth, a man of the centre, put it after the assassination of the democratic politician and industrialist Rathenau in 1922).[2] Whether a liberal view of institutions has a chance against such forces, is an open question; but it must be tried if we do not want to lose both security and freedom.[3]

This is heavy and even opaque language which will become lighter and clearer as we go along. Let us then return to Berlin for a moment, and to the lessons of the experience for law and order. One is that lawlessness did not last. Perhaps it cannot last. It is a fleeting moment of transition rather than a long-term state of affairs. To be sure, in Beirut it seems to have lasted a long time; but then we are told that in Lebanon the apparent war of all against all is in fact a highly structured affair. This is *a fortiori* the case in Belfast. Civil war is something quite different from the erosion and eventual decomposition of law and order. Wherever such decomposition occurs, it creates a vacuum which not only does not endure, but which seems to invite rather elementary norms and sanctions and a very crude exercise of power. One of the miseries of anomy is that it augurs ill for liberty. It creates a state of fear while it lasts, and calls for a state of tyranny as a remedy.[4] Once the

Hobbesian problem of order arises, the solution tends to be Hobbesian as well.[5]

Another lesson of the Berlin story is that it provides a perspective on the dimension of the problem. The fall of Berlin in 1945 produced one of those absolute situations which are as instructive about the human condition as they are rare in human history. Whatever may be felt, or found about the erosion of law and order in the free societies of the world today, is in fact but a rather small step in the direction of a condition which people have lived to see in Berlin, and perhaps in Beirut and Belfast as well. By and large, even New Yorkers live in a fairly orderly world in which there are no deserted army stores to take meat from, and where one cannot simply walk out of bookshops with volumes of romantic poetry. There is no total discontinuity of public authorities, nor is there a temporary suspension of their operation. There are laws, and there is order.

What then do we mean when we speak of an erosion of law and order today? Is there in fact such a process at all? And if there is, does it have to lead all the way to Anomia? Could it not be a temporary aberration, or at any rate a reversible trend? These are big questions. They demand clear answers, and we shall try to give them. However, as we embark on this venture, I must ask the indulgence of those who are experts in the vast literature on deviance, delinquency and their causes. The following argument will be quite elementary, and it is based on equally elementary facts. My only justification is that sometimes simplicity allows one to cut through a tangle of complications and get to the heart of the matter.

The other day I found, in one of those glossy magazines displayed in expensive hotel rooms for the edification of weary travellers, an "Editorial" which ran as follows:

"Have we by now got used to the fact that no woman can go out alone at night, and that our property is no longer safe?

Every one of us lives every day with the fear that ruthless criminals drive up in a van in bright daylight and empty our houses. Yet if we are not alerted by this happening to someone we know, we repress the problem.

Every year, 4.3 million criminal acts occur in the country—an alarming and frightening figure, though only the tip of the iceberg, because the dark figure is many times higher. The cruelty and misery brought about by crime is almost unimaginable, yet pain and suffering are largely ignored.

In the last ten years, the number of criminal acts has increased by 70 per cent., with theft and robbery heading the list. But the number of policemen was only raised by 35 per cent. Small police stations had to be closed for cost reasons; in some cases, the police have to travel twenty kilometres to get to the scene of a crime. By that time the perpetrators have of course long disappeared.

Detection succeeds in only 45 per cent. of all cases, otherwise the police fumble in a fog of detection. Judging by these figures, the state is no longer able to look after our safety and the protection of our property. Such observations require solutions. A first step is of course the employment of more police forces, but their training should be improved as well. Not least should we improve our attitude to the rule of law. Our youngsters keep on referring to 'pigs'; our 'friend and helper' has an image which has sunk below zero.

The changes needed cost money. The minister of interior refers to the empty coffers of the state. My view is that subsidies for many a branch of industry are misspent. Here, every year a financial potential is poured out like a warm rain which could be spent for more safety. Nor can security within be allowed to collapse for lack of manpower, for unemployed youths will surely be grateful to find government-paid jobs.

We all want to live in safety and peace again. It must not happen that the citizen has to live in permanent fear for his property. Or do we want a 'nightwatchman' state which displays and tolerates laissez-faire attitudes towards criminals?"[6]

The temptation is great to pour irony over such statements. The facts are misleading; figures of percentage increases of criminal acts in general over an arbitrary period of time and in one country (in this case, Germany) tell us very little. The conclusions are overstated; it is simply not true that anybody can drive up in a van anywhere and empty houses. The remedies are implausible; even apart from the curious notion that unemployed youths would provide cheap policemen, increasing the police force in line with increases in crime is simply an expensive distraction.

Yet perhaps we should not judge our editorialist too harshly. For one thing, as one is tempted to cast doubt on the fear of others about law and order, it is as well to remember the stricture implicit in the New York quip: a liberal is a person who has not yet been mugged?[7] For another, the hotel journalist represents a rather mild variant of a posture for which there are many cruder and more vicious examples in popular newspapers as well as campaign speeches, to say nothing of pubs and clubs. He has in the process raised the important question of the kind of government we want (though he seems slightly confused about the alternatives): Do we want a soft social state which allows crime to get out of hand—or a tougher state which clamps down on crime and keeps the needy busy by a Darwinian struggle for economic survival? Or is there a third alternative? Robert Nozick's "minimal state" perhaps which, at least in its realm, is not a "nightwatchman's state," though it lets people do their thing elsewhere?[8]

But above all, the fact that the editorialist can hope to meet with an appreciative response among his readers, is significant. They are of course comfortably-off middle-class people; but the response would reverberate among many who are less well-to-do. There is a widespread perception of serious problems of law and order. This has been documented by opinion research, by the appeal of certain political platforms, by the flourishing of the security business. Many people feel frightened, whether they have been mugged yet or not.

And there are reasons. The facts are complex, though ultimately unambiguous. Here are some of them, relating to the developed and free countries of the world about which we have fairly reliable information. In many of these countries, there has been a major increase in crimes of violence against the person since the mid-1950s and even more dramatically, since the 1960s. In some, the rate of murders has doubled during this period. This is true in the United States, in Britain, in Germany, the Netherlands, Sweden. An even more general and pronounced trend is evident with respect to assault, robbery with violence, and possibly rape. In many countries and most large cities the incidence of these serious crimes is, in the 1980s three times that or more of what it was in the 1950s.[9]

The increase in crimes against property is still more dramatic. There are several big countries in which rates of robbery have at least quadrupled since the 1950s, and some, including Britain, where they have grown by an even larger factor. The rise appears to be particularly rapid in the 1980s. The evidence on theft is for a variety of reasons somewhat less convincing, but from available statistics and studies, the probability is high that there has been a similar increase.

During the same 30 years, there has probably been a considerable growth of the number of persons who can be said to live on crime. Leon Radzinowicz and Joan King report the findings of surveys according to which "very few people—less than one in ten—have never been guilty of lawbreaking at all. And several of the studies show that well over half confessed to at least one crime for which, if convicted as adults, they could have been sent to prison."[10] More significantly, prosperity has brought with it new categories of crime, such as thefts of and from cars. But above all, there is the growing importance of drugs, and drug-related crime, as well as the number of people who are able to make a living out of a commodity which has a higher added value at each stage than almost any legal good.

With the growing number of crimes and criminals, there is also a growing number of victims. Clearly, New York is exceptional, where "it has been estimated that any citizen has six chances in ten, during the course of his or her life, of being the victim of murder, rape, assault or robbery."[11] Also, so-called victimisation surveys are too recent to permit conclusive statements of trends. On the other hand, there is enough evidence to state, at least for the United States and Britain, a growth in the number of victims of crimes of violence against the person or of crimes against property in the last 30 years.[12]

These are facts. To this extent, in other words, Radzinowicz's reference to a "relentless upsurge in crime" cannot be denied nor can Michael Zander's statement be disputed: "There is no doubt that the public's anxiety about the growing menace of crime is well founded."[13] This has to be emphasised in view of the existence of a school of socio-ideology which advances a curious set of arguments against citing the facts. They are dismissed by some as irrelevant: "The law and order issue serves to deflect public attention from more pressing issues, like death, destruction, war, torture and starvation."[14] Others try to make them disappear in a mist of interpretation:

increasing crime rates merely tell us that people own more goods, or that "we have made it easier for lower class persons . . . to move freely about the city," or simply that there are more young people.[15] Again others follow the old adage that it is not the murderer but his victim who is guilty and recommend "better home security, car steering locks, entry-phones and the like" in the place of imprisonment which "has only a marginal role in crime prevention at best."[16] It is worth noting however that none of these attempts actually dispute the facts; they merely do not face them. Yet we have to face them if we want to understand the world in which we are living.

This is not to detract from some necessary qualifications. Comparative studies demonstrate that it is misleading to speak loosely of developed free countries. Even apart from Japan, there are considerable differences between them. International comparisons of crime figures are notoriously difficult; but some differences stand out.[17] The facts which we have cited apply more clearly to the United States than to Canada; they apply to Britain but to France only with respect to crimes against property, and that to a lesser extent; they apply to Germany but apparently not to Italy, to Sweden but in a much more limited way to the Netherlands. This may well be true also for the rest of our analysis. We may thus be talking above all of Britain, Germany, the United States rather than France, Italy, Switzerland. Indeed, such differences raise questions of analysis themselves: what is it that seems to make France relatively immune to the upsurge in crimes of violence against the person? Why are rates of homicide relatively stable in Austria, Belgium, France, Italy, Switzerland, whereas they have at least doubled in Britain and the United States?

The other major qualification is that even where we have longitudinal comparisons, the evidence does not take us back very far. We are fortunate if we can find comparable data from 1900 to the present which enable us to assess the effect of the wars of this century on crime.[18] There are some isolated American studies about apparent increases in crimes of violence at the time of the War of Independence, and again after the Civil War, which lead at least one author to the general observation that it is "extreme disorganization, or anomie," "the dislocation and virtual collapse of the institutional order of the total society," which result in rising rates of crime.[19] Berlin again! We shall return to the subject presently.

But what about Barbara Tuchman's *Distant Mirror* of the fourteenth century which she described with more than one eye on our own time? "The 14th century suffered so many 'strange and great perils and adversities' (in the words of a contemporary) that its disorders cannot be traced to any one cause; they were the hoofprints of more than the four horsemen of St. John's vision, which had now become seven— plague, war, taxes, brigandage, bad government, insurrection, and schism in the Church."[20] Barbara Tuchman is not only gloomy. After apocalypse, there is a new dawn. "Times were to grow worse over the next fifty years until at some imperceptible moment, by some mysterious chemistry, energies were refreshed, ideas broke out of the mould of the Middle Ages into new realms, and humanity found itself re-directed."[21] Are we really passing through a similar phase of "apocalypse"? And is the erosion of law and order one of the hoofprints of the horsemen of the twentieth century?

More to the point perhaps: what about England in the seventeenth century? It was clearly no accident that the old idea of the social contract was rediscovered at the time of the great disorders, nor are the vivid descriptions of the state of nature mere products of the imagination of Thomas Hobbes or John Locke. "The shocks of civil war and regicide set men debating about institutions and traditions that had been instinctively obeyed for centuries."[22] One would dearly like to know what other indications there were of decomposition and impending change, and more particularly what the state of law and order was in the decades between Cromwell's assumption of power and the "glorious revolution."

These are ambitious questions, not only because historical evidence to answer them is hard to come by, but also because, like the experience of Berlin in 1945, they suggest a dimension of the problem which may be far from what is happening in the free countries of the world today.

Here, a more modest and also more rigorous analysis is needed before the facts make any sense at all. We have, as it were, illustrated the process of the erosion of law and order by a few indisputable facts. But what do the facts tell us? The answer may seem simple enough, but it is not. As we examine the possibilities we encounter a number of surprises.

Does the erosion of law and order mean that more people are transgressing the norms established by due constitutional process? Or that more norms are violated? At first sight, this may seem plausible, but as so often, it is useful to have a second look. There is *deviance*. This is not a very startling observation. Some societies claim to have done away with all crime, and since there cannot be what must not be, they do not publish police statistics, thereby muddying the waters of comparative analysts. However, the Soviet Union cannot deceive us in this respect. We know for a fact that its definition of deviance is among the narrowest, and its treatment of deviants among the cruellest in the world. It includes the helpless victims of political pyschiatry as well as the modern slaves of Gulag and many who are banned within as well as some who are banned from the country. The German Democratic Republic, along with other East European countries, naturally follows suit in this respect as in others. Yet while there are no official crime figures, a textbook of criminal law (with restricted circulation) states somewhat pompously in 1984: "Delinquency in the GDR represents today a phenomenon of a relatively massive order of magnitude." [23]

I do not know whether there is such a phenomenon as a "natural rate of crime" in analogy to the economists' "natural rate of unemployment." If there is, it probably has to be adjusted as often as that of unemployment, and usually upwards. But whatever the differences of history and culture, it is doubtful whether deviance can be pushed below a certain level, and questionable whether one should try. In any case, a fairly significant level of crime is compatible with all societies, and notably with those which are vigorous and free.

Thus we have to rule out the extremes. The official Soviet line is simply suspicious; the facts are different. On the other hand, Berlin 1945 is clearly outside the range of what might be called, normal. But between the extremes of deceptive order and total disorder there is a wide range of real conditions. We may sense that the perceptions and facts with which we have started here describe a state of affairs which is no longer normal, that it is unusual and perhaps unstable; but short of much better comparative and longitudinal evidence, there is no way to substantiate such claims. The fact that many people—many more people than 30 year ago—act contrary to fairly elementary norms, raises questions, but permits no conclusions.

So we are left with our question what exactly the erosion of law and order might mean. Is it perhaps that many acts in contravention of norms remain unknown, or at any rate unreported? The latter addition is intended to spell out that we are here concerned with *ignorance* (as I shall call it) on the part of authorities about acts which would have to be classified as criminal. Leon Radzinowicz is "inclined to believe that the criminal of today is more likely to remain hidden than his predecessor some forty or seventy years ago"[24]; he cites the anonymity of life and the mobility of people as supporting evidence. His guess that only 15 per cent. of all crimes ever become fully known has since been largely confirmed by surveys of victims which suggest that "at least eighty per cent. of crime goes unreported, and this figure is almost certainly a gross underestimate."[25] Of course, there is no way in which the historical assertion that this figure is "expanding," can be proven.

People, including scholarly authors, get much agitated about ignorance, and they are undoubtedly right. Yet there is an important proviso. Heinrich Popitz (on whose analysis of the "normative construction of society" I am drawing here in more ways than one) has written a little piece called, "On the Preventive Effect of Ignorance."[26] Using William Thackeray's "On Being Found Out" to illustrate that if all crimes were detected not only the emperor but most ordinary men too would have no clothes—did I not confess to once stealing romantic poetry myself?—Popitz argues with beautiful irony the important point that no system of norms could bear full knowledge of every breach. "A society which was to uncover every case of deviance, would ruin the validity of its norms."[27] "Norms cannot stand the searchlight, they need a little duskiness."[28] Again, this is not to say that we have got the quantity, or indeed the social stratification of ignorance right. It may well be that there is too much ignorance in the wrong places. But a large question mark remains over any conclusion that is drawn from such guesswork.

What has been called, ignorance, is of course the really dark figure of crime. However, there is also a *dark figure* in the narrower sense which has to do with the statement that known acts contrary to norms remain undetected. Is this perhaps what we mean when we talk about the erosion of law and order? Is there, in other words, a dramatic decline in detection rates and a corresponding rise in the dark figure of crime? We obviously know rather more about the dark figure than about ignorance, although what we seem to know is both disputed and variously interpreted. It appears for example that detection rates for recorded cases of theft are relatively low; official British estimates of 40 per cent. may well be on the high side. Reported murder on the other hand is, according to published figures, found out in more the 80 per cent. of all cases.[29] It has been argued that the more vicious a crime is, the higher the chance of detection[30]; but whether this applies to rape, or even to assault is doubtful. In both cases, the victims (women; young people who are themselves close to the criminal scene) are often unlikely to report the crime, and if it is reported, unwilling to help in detecting the offender. Thus, all we know is that there are significant differences in the dark figure of different crimes. Once again, the extremes must be ruled out. Complete detection of all known crimes is unlikely in any category, and a zero rate of detection would be, to say the least, a little suspicious. But once again also there is a wide range which must be regarded, in the absence of clear and quantifiable evidence to the contrary, as normal.

Is there then no problem of law and order? the thrust of our argument so far is that it is not easy to pinpoint the problem. It is certainly not enough to cite increasing rates of crime, growing ignorance and a rising dark figure, and then say *voila!* as if it was self-evident that these increases indicate a serious secular process. For all we know, they may be well within a range of normalcy, and at worst temporary or conjunctural aberrations which will return to lower levels as certain passing social or economic conditions change. Rather this might be the case, unless one other condition is present which defines the real problem of law and order: acts contrary to norms remain unsanctioned. The increasing absence of effective sanctions, if such exists, is the true meaning of the erosion of law and order. It not only describes the phenomenon more precisely than the transgression of norms or lack of knowledge about it, but it also removes it from the conjunctural and contingent. If violations of norms are not sanctioned, or no longer sanctioned systematically, they become themselves systematic. As we pursue such statements we are soon led into the treacherous yet fertile field of *anomy*. I am using the ancient (the *Oxford Dictionary* says, "obsolete") word rather than the term *anomie* of modern social science for what Lambarde described in 1591 as "bringing disorder, doubt and uncertainty over all."[31]

The notion that acts in contravention of norms remain unsanctioned, is itself quite complex. The story begins somewhere between ignorance and non-detection, when crimes become known to the police but are not recorded. "Sorry, madam, but we really are too busy to come round when no one was hurt and all that was stolen was an old television set." There are layers of what might be called, depending on one's perspective, the withholding of sanctions, or exemption from sanctions (*Sanktionsverzicht*[32]). There is the exemption from sanctions out of weakness, as when the police turns a blind eye on known delinquents. A lower readiness to apply sanctions may become part and parcel of a prevailing social climate. There is the deliberate waiver of sanctions, for first offenders, young offenders. There is the whole process of the emasculation of sanctions, so that potential offenders know that a life sentence cannot mean more than 15 years of detention (as in Sweden). There is the inability to cope with offences because they are too numerous, or too many people are involved in them at one time. These issues will accompany us throughout. They are all examples of *impunity*, and I shall argue that it is in this area that the normative validity of a social order is decided. Impunity, or the systematic waiver of sanctions, links crime and the exercise of authority. It tells us something about the legitimacy of an order. It is an indicator of decomposition as well as change and innovation. The growing incidence of impunity leads us to the core of the modern social problem.

In the paper which I have already quoted, Popitz argues that sanctioning breaches of norms must not exceed a limited quantitative range. If an employer, a parent, a superior in any context tries to sanction every transgression which he or she witness out of the corner of their eyes, they will destroy the effectiveness of all sanctions. "A superior who cannot pretend to be dumb in some situations, is dumb."[33] But here, more than in the case of the dark figure, the boundary between the preventive and the destructive effect of inaction is precarious. Waving the disciplinary code every time a principal is displeased, and hiding it in the bottom drawer in the hope that nobody remembers it, may well both lead to the same result, anomy. Anomy ensues if a large, and growing number of breaches of norms are known and reported, but not sanctioned.

The term, anomy, was of course introduced into modern social science by Émile Durkheim in his attempt to classify, and perhaps explain, suicide. Man is bound by social bonds which produce "a conscience superior to his own, the superiority of which he feels." "But when society is disturbed by some painful crisis or by beneficent but abrupt transitions, it is momentarily incapable of exercising this influence; thence come the sudden rises in the curve of suicides."[34] "Anomic suicide" is notably a concomitant of economic crises, including the permanent crisis of the industrial revolution. Durkheim's book, *Suicide*, was first published in 1897. His two major French successors as analysts of suicide, Maurice Halbwachs (*Les causes du suicide*, 1930), and Jean Baechler (*Les suicides*, 1975) did not much like the notion of anomy, nor did Jack D. Douglas in his *Social Meanings of Suicide* (1967). As one sociologist put it in connection with explanations of crime: "The rise and fall of anomie theory were both unusually speedy happenings."[35]

But then such theoretical fashions are always a little suspicious. It is often as well to ignore them and concentrate on the substance of attempts at explanation. Durkheim was curiously ambiguous in his use of the term, anomy. Despite his sociological programme of structural analysis, he wavered in this case between a rather superficial socio-economic analysis and a somewhat dubious psychological classification. Halbwachs took him to task for the former and pointed out that it is by no means always true that economic crises produce increases in suicide rates, and that those most affected by them are in fact unlikely candidates for suicide. Baechler who cannot speak of "the anomie so dear to Durkheim" without irony, makes a point which is more important in our context when he says about "anomic suicide": "I do not see the need to refute such vague and general arguments, the explanatory interest of which seems to me to be exactly nil."[36] Baechler is saying that the unique and dramatic individual act of suicide cannot be explained by reference to a vaguely defined social condition.

In an important sense this also applies to crime where Radzinowicz has made a similar point: "Definitions and criteria of anomie have been vague, sometimes conflicting, sometimes circular. . . . Attempts to test its impact on criminality have not shown a simple relationship."[37] It should therefore be stated clearly and without reservation that we are not introducing the term, anomy, to explain individual criminal acts. There probably is no such thing as "anomic suicide", and there certainly is no "anomic crime". Anomy is a social condition which can give rise to many kinds of behaviour, as did the fall of Berlin in 1945. The invocation of such a condition does not invalidate the complex explanations of delinquency offered by criminologists nor does it add to them. The connection between anomy and crime is not causal. Anomy provides a background condition in which crime *rates* are likely to be high; and the analysis of crime leads us to a better understanding of anomy. Moreover, the process of anomy has its own interest in the context of socio-political analysis. It is introduced here to advance an argument about social order and freedom, not about crime and punishment.

Anomy then is not a state of mind, but a state of society.[38] But what kind of state is it? Robert Merton has tried, in his famous essays on "Social Structure and Anomie," to render the term more precise: "Anomie is then conceived as a breakdown in the cultural structure, occurring particularly when there is an acute disjunction between the cultural norms and goals, and the socially structured capacities of members of the group to act in accord with them."[39] In other words, if people are led by deeply engrained assumptions of their culture, such as the American dream of unlimited opportunities, to expect personal success, but in fact social and economic factors prevent them from getting on, disorientation and uncertainty set in. Anthony Giddens has pursued this theme and applied Merton's distinction of culture and society—or, as Giddens prefers to say with David Lockwoods terms, of "social integration" and "system integration"—to the original theme, suicide. It is a pity that Giddens chooses to seek what he calls a "point of articulation between social structural and psychological factors," that is a translation of a social condition to individual action ("anomic suicide"). The more plausible statement of his is this: "Anomie, as a general condition of social structure, sets a general 'background' making for disjunction between social norms and the goals and aspirations which individuals hold."[40]

Sorting out these various definitions might well

lead one to abandon the concept altogether. It seems to tempt people to take on too much at one time. Durkheim (and in his succession others, including Giddens) misleadingly suggests that a state of social decomposition must lead to certain individual courses of action. Merton equally misleadingly offers a possible partial explanation of social decomposition—the disjunction between cultural goals and social means—and in the process overburdens as well as confuses a notion which is in the first instance no more that the description of an extreme social state, and which may well involve the decomposition of both culture and society.

Yet it would be a pity to abandon the word, anomy, which is so strong and has been so close historically to the description of the opposite condition to social order. Perhaps we can avoid misleading connotations by a slight change of language and speak of Anomia (in analogy to Utopia) instead. Anomia is a social condition in which the norms which govern people's behaviour have lost their validity. One guarantee of such validity consists in the clear and present force of sanctions. Where impunity prevails, the effectiveness of norms is in jeopardy. In this sense, Anomia describes a state of affairs in which breaches of norms go unpunished.

This is a state of extreme uncertainty in which no one knows what behaviour to expect from others in given situations. There is a view of society underlying such statements, or at any rate a terminology, which needs to be made explicit. Human societies are sets of valid norms which make behaviour predictable. Norms are valid not primarily because they are actually observed, or in some absolute sense morally right, but because their breach is punished by sanctions. In a given social situation, we know what behaviour to expect from others because we know that if they behave differently they will be punished. Their effectiveness links norms through sanctions with power, or rather, with institutionalised power, authority. Sanctions imply an agency which is able to enforce them. In this perspective, the social contract, that is the fictitious base of social order, is of necessity both a "contract of association" and a "contract of domination."[41]

The related concepts of norm, sanction and authority not only help describe society, but their varieties would serve to identify open and totalitarian, traditional and modern societies as well as order and anomy. Yet to understand the latter, one dimension has to be added. We said that *one* guarantee of the validity of norms consists in sanctions. Effectiveness is however only one side of the coin. The other brings us back to Durkheim's "bonds" which are "not physical, but moral; that is, social," and to his notion of a conscience superior to our own.[42] Underneath social structure there are moulds of human behaviour which we may call, cultural. They too are changeable, though they change more slowly than social structures; the deeper bond between mother and child is not immediately affected by changes in the age of suffrage, or even of divorce law and rules of inheritance. Among such cultural moulds are not only those deeper bonds which we shall call, ligatures, but also moral beliefs and other ingredients of people's conscience. They add an element of morality to the validity of norms. Norms are valid in other words if and when they are both effective and moral, that is (believed to be) real and (believed to be) right. It will readily be seen that there are relations between this terminology and the concepts of legality (the positive effectiveness of norms) and legitimacy (the coincidence of effectiveness and morality).

Anomia then is a condition in which both the social effectiveness and the cultural morality of norms tend towards zero. This in turn means that sanctions are no longer applied and that people's conscience is, in Durkheim's words, "incapable of exercising [its] influence." Given the role of authority in backing up sanctions, anomy is also anarchy. This is important, especially since it is not true, or rather often not believed to be true the other way round. Many well-meaning anarchists dream of a world in which all authority has been dispensed with, though few accept that this would also be a world without norms. The anarchist dream is one of self-sustaining norms without prisons, police and politicians. The dream is misguided, even dangerously so if it leads to attempts to implement it. Norms, sanctions and power are indissolubly linked. But one can see why it should be tempting to decouple them. It would be nice to live in a world of law and order without the institutions of law and order. Nice but impractical, is how one might describe anarchy. Anomia, on the other hand, is like Utopia not so much impractical as unreal. It may well be that, as Robert Merton suspected, there is a "strain toward anomie" in modern societies.[43] Indeed there is perhaps a strain towards Anomia in all human societies.

After all, why should people submit to norms, sanctions and authority rather than cheat the categorical imperative in their own interest? But similarly, there is a strain towards Utopia in people's thinking. The dream of perfect order is ineradicable even in social thought. Yet Utopia cannot be, however much detail Parsonian sociology has added to it; men are forever imperfect and history is therefore forever on the move.[44] And Anomia cannot last, even if there are approximations like Berlin 1945, or the orgasm of revolution.

Lambarde put it well; Anomia "brings disorder, doubt and uncertainty over all." People can no longer predict whether their neighbour is going to kill them or give them his horse. Norms no longer seem to exist, or if they are invoked, they turn out to be toothless. All sanctions seem to have withered away. This in turn refers to the disappearance of power or, more technically, a re-transformation of legitimate authority into crude and arbitrary power. This is hardly a state in which anyone would wish to live. It is likely that men could not survive in it for long.

But men can live on the road to Anomia which is in fact the condition of some contemporary societies. We have begun with statements about crime and its victims. They give pointers, but prove little. We have then tried to make sense of the figures and discovered that the road to Anomia would be a road along which sanctions are progressively weakened. They are withheld by those in charge; individuals and groups are exempted from them. Impunity becomes the order of the day. It remains for us to ask, and answer the question whether there are any convincing indications of this process of declining sanctions, for only if this is the case does our central thesis stand up. Are there kinds of breaches of norms and segments of society which the arm of the law does not reach? Is there a systematic decomposition of sanctions in important areas of social life? Are there, as it were, "no-go areas" in the social as well as the physical sense where anything may happen and anomy reigns? I believe that there are and would cite in support four features of modern societies which bring out the deeper problem of law and order.

The first of these features may well be the least important. It is that certain crimes, certain violations of norms, have become no-go areas, as it were. This is of course not a new phenomenon. It can probably be said that most fundamental changes of norms are preceded by periods in which sanctions are no longer applied systematically. If abortion, or homosexuality, are no longer prosecuted, this does not signify an intrinsic weakness of social order, but a process of changing values which will sooner or later be translated into an adjustment of valid norms. In this sense, it is perfectly normal that there should be no-go areas for the sanctioning instances.

But a line must be drawn between changing norms and processes of decomposition. Two major examples illustrate the difference. There can be little doubt that in most modern societies many incidents of theft are no longer punished. We have seen that the dark figure is particularly high in the case of theft; it is above 40 per cent. Experts suspect, and surveys of victims confirm, that ignorance is also particularly great; the overwhelming majority of thefts are not recorded. There is in addition the phenomenon of deliberate ignorance to which we have referred; thefts are reported, but not investigated, let alone prosecuted. If and when they are prosecuted, the result is more often than not what Zander calls the "acquittal of the guilty"; in Britain alone, ten thousand such cases are known to occur each year.[45] If this is a sign of change, it signifies not the arrival of new valid norms but of normlessness, anomy.

The same is true for that important feature of many modern societies, the black economy. A German tax lawyer created a storm when he argued on fairly conclusive evidence at a conference of tax accountants in 1984 that 90 per cent. of all Germans are tax dodgers and explained this fact by "the non-punishment of the many."[46] "We are not a nation of criminals," the president of the accountants' body insisted in his reply. He may be right in the sense that in the absence of sanctions, the very term, criminal, ceases to have any meaning. But then the waiver of sanctions against tax avoidance is a sign of decomposition rather than change. If 10 per cent. or more of the gross national product are produced in the shadows of the unofficial economy, this may be an expression of people's vitality and their ability to escape the iron cage of bondage of modern bureaucratised states, but it is also a sign of anomy. People take the law into their own hands. (They do so more in some countries than in others; from this point of view, the stability of Italian crime figures takes on a very different complexion.) The law no longer works.

A second social no-go area presents the most serious problem of all, and will accompany us throughout these lectures. It is that of youth. In all modern societies, young people account for by far the major part of all crimes, and notably serious crimes including homicide, rape, assault and robbery. The facts are shocking from any point of view. "People under twenty-one account for something like half of those found guilty of the traditional crimes." "In England boys are up to ten times as likely to be dealt with for criminal offence as full grown men"; and in America, similarly, "the population aged fourteen to twenty-four [is] the group from which most criminals are drawn."[47] In England and Wales, no fewer than eight per cent. of all 14- to 16-year-olds were "found guilty of, or cautioned for, serious offences" in one single year (1978). By contrast, fewer than one-third of one per cent. of all those who are 50 years old and older were found guilty of such offences. Moreover, the rate for older men has not changed much over the years, whereas among the young, there has been a major increase. For example, in England and Wales, the rate of serious crimes among 14- to 16-year-olds was one-third of what it is today in the late 1960s.[48]

There is no shortage of similarly striking data. However, in terms of our definition of anomia, the critical fact is that the system of sanctions associated with norms has been softened significantly and to some extent suspended outright in the case of the young. So far as those under 17 years of age are concerned, conditional discharges, supervision orders, and attendance centre orders account for more than 50 per cent. of all sentences for serious offences (in England and Wales, 1978). A closer analysis of sentencing figures shows in all modern countries of the free world a clear tendency to exempt young offenders from sanctions. At the very least we can state that while the incidence of serious crimes has increased significantly among those under 20, there has been a systematic tendency to reduce sanctions for the young. Whether we can also state that with the—because of the?—waiver of sanctions against the young, juvenile delinquency has increased, may be another matter. It takes us back to criminology, and the individual consequences of anomy. However, even if there are one or two links missing in the story, there remains a worrying paradox.

A third no-go area is that for which the notion was originally invented. Although the police will deny that there are any areas which they avoid deliberately and systematically, many members of the public know—or believe they know, which is sufficient—that there are parts of cities, as well as for example subways at certain hours, to which one does not go. If members of the public do not go because they expect to be mugged, this is a clear indication that an area has become exempt from the normal process of maintaining law and order. There are indications that such no-go areas are spreading. The clearest sign is that members of the public have begun to set up their own system of sanctions, or rather, since it is precisely the sanctions which are missing, their system of counter-violence. In the United States in particular, the hiring of private guards and the setting-up of vigilante groups have become more wide-spread, often under the euphemism of community self-help. The recent case of the man who shot several youths late at night in a New York subway train made headlines because public approval was initially even translated into a Grand Jury decision not to indict the killer for attempted murder or man-slaughter.[49] It is widely accepted that in no-go areas anything goes.

Some territorial no-go areas are less visible than subway trains or parts of large cities; they are institutions or organisations, schools, universities, enterprises, administrative offices, often with their own codes of discipline which are no longer applied. In inner-city schools, it is sometimes the teachers rather than pupils who live in a state of fear. Universities find it notoriously difficult to use their disciplinary codes; there is an unspoken assumption that behaviour which would be regarded as intolerable else-where will be tolerated. In many organisations, a combination of employment protection legislation and managerial appeasement makes it virtually impossible to use the sanction of expulsion or of firing people. In all these cases, a general climate according to which sanctions are somehow a bad thing is translated into impunity and impotence.

It is worth reflecting for a moment on the notion which we have used here almost as a matter of course, no-go area. Article One of the social contract (if such a thing exists) stipulates that norms are upheld by sanctions which are imposed by proper authorities. In other words, it establishes a monopoly of violence in the hands of authorised agencies and individuals. But today we realize that Max Weber's definition of the state in these terms is by no means a matter of course.[50] There is not only unauthorised violence—which, as we have argued throughout, may be awkward and painful, but is not as such the problem of law and order—but there are parts of society like the young, the inner cities, and certain kinds of breaches of norms where the state has all but abandoned its monopoly. *Mutatis mutandis* the same can be said for particular organisations and institutions. This is what no-go areas really mean. If however privatisation is driven to this extreme, the result is partial anomy. The observations recounted here certainly justify our speaking of modern societies being on the road to Anomia.

A fourth set of facts has to be added to the three which we have mentioned so far. If breaches of norms become sufficiently massive, the application of sanctions becomes by the same token extremely difficult and sometimes impossible. Mutiny, riot, rebellion, revolt, insurrection, violent demonstrations, mass occupations of buildings, vicious strike pickets and other forms of civil disorder somehow defy a sanctioning process which is essentially geared to individuals and identifiable small groups. It is all very well to map out police tactics of dispersal, segmentation, the arrest of leaders, and to demand that "the police and the courts must see to it that all those who were guilty of serious offences are prosecuted"; but the very next sentences of Raymond Momboisse's manual on *Riots, Revolts and Insurrections* betray the impotence of sanctions at times of riot: "Further, every effort must be made to prevent further incitement of public passion, ensuring that an atmosphere has been established in which law and order clearly prevail maintained by the police." This should be achieved by careful analysis and corrective action, meetings of all groups on neutral ground, press coverage and affirmative action "to rectify the conditions which precipitated the riot."[51]

The examples are many. There is clearly something pathetic about the arrest of 39 soccer hooligans if hundreds were involved in breaking up terraces, attacking rival fans and finally the police, looting shops and injuring innocent bystanders; and it is not surprising if of the 39, 35 have to be released the next morning because it is impossible to bring charges against them as individuals. Nor are we astonished to learn that the one "fan" who was caught physically assaulting a player on the field, was sentenced to one year's detention and immediately released on remand.[52] Similar stories could be told about violent picketing during the 1984/85 miners' strike in Britain, or the civil disorders of the New York blackout in 1977, and of Brixton and Toxteth in 1981, or of the anti-nuclear demonstrations in Germany in 1983/84. The examples, however different they may be in their immediate objectives, the composition of the crowds involved, and the degree of violence used have a significant process of aggravation in common. The events in question start as something more or less legal, a football game, a strike, a demonstration. They then become more tense and occasionally violent, often in the form of clashes between groups. But the crucial moment is when mass action and occasional violence turn against the authorities. Lord Scarman's description of the Brixton disorders can stand for many others: "The disorder was not initially a riot. . . . The critical moment was when the crowd turned and stoned the police."[53] The rather endearing English legal definition of riots as violent crowd action which "alarms at least one person of reasonable firmness and courage"[54] cannot deceive one over two significant facts. One is that sanctions become ineffective; during the soccer riot alluded to earlier, specially trained police dogs took flight from the vicious crowd. The other, related one is that authority itself becomes the issue and is at least temporarily suspended.

This raises a question which we have encountered in a variety of guises and which must at least be brought into the open. When is disorder a riot, and when is it a revolution? When, in other words, are we talking about Anomia, and when about change, albeit to Utopia? In terms of the day of action, there is little apparent difference between riots and revolutions. More than that, there are times when public disorder can tip either way; Paris in May 1968 is the obvious example. In terms of the outcome of action, there is a clear difference. Riots die down, even if they last for days and flare up time and again; revolutions lead to the overthrow of a government and a regime. This means that with respect to the underlying forces, there is a crucial distinction. In the case of revolutions, the powder keg of a revolutionary situation has to be present into which the spark of Utopian hope is thrown; in the case of riots, igniting the powder is but a display of fireworks by comparison.

Whatever frustrations may seek expression in riotous behaviour, they are not sustained demands for power by suppressed social classes and their spokesmen. Riots are massive individual acts of protest; revolutions are genuinely collective manifestations of a demand for change. Riots are essentially destructive; revolutions have a constructive element that sustains them. In this sense, riots belong into the context of anomy, revolutions into that of change.

In our context, the question remains whether unmanageable riots have increased in frequency and viciousness. If one compares the 1970s and early 1980s with the 1950s and early 1960s, this is probably the case at least in the countries to which this analysis applies above all. If one takes a longer historical perspective, as one must before one reaches firm conclusions, the result is more doubtful. Both the reports by the United States National Advisory Commission on Civil Disorders of 1968, and by Lord Scarman on the Brixton Disorders of 1981 concentrate on the issue at hand, race and inner-city deprivation.[55] Other subjects, notably industrial relations, have led to riots in the past. In Germany, the Weimar Republic in its later years was clearly on the road to Anomia. Indeed, in many countries, the time of the Great Depression was also a time of civil disorder. It is therefore with some hesitation that I would state that two recent developments are relevant in our context. One is that more people than ever before have found it necessary to express their frustrations by crowd action ranging from peaceful demonstrations to riots. Perhaps, this is simply a by-product of greater participation and "democratisation." The other development is that the frequency of incidents which demonstrate the weakness of the sanctions of the law contributes to a feeling that one can get away with crowd delinquency; there is doubt in the effectiveness, and perhaps even the legitimacy of prevailing norms and authorities. But that is of course begging our main question.

There are other observations which could and perhaps should have been made. Organised crime is one of the phenomena which in some societies cast serious doubt on the state's monopoly of violence. Terrorism claims considerable support by playing on the precarious boundary between crime and change, riot and revolution. But we have already moved a long way from the preoccupations and realities ordinarily associated with the concept of law and order. It is therefore time to summarise the initial argument and tie up one remaining loose end.

There are times when all predictability seems to fade from social life. Fears of a breakdown of law and order have to do with this nightmare. That such fears are present in many of the advanced societies of the free world, is beyond doubt. Their presence is in itself an indication of problems of social order. Moreover, such fears are founded in fact. Although as such they mean little, these facts show a considerable increase in serious crimes in the last 30 years. The significance of the facts becomes evident if we place them in context. It is apparent that they are not quirks of conjuncture, but the result of a process of weakening sanctions with all that follows from such a process not only for the effectiveness of social order but also for the legitimacy of authority. Major social trends

about which there can be no serious dispute confirm
the rapid spread of impunity. In this sense, we are on
the road to Anomia.

Why this should be so, will be the subject of the
next two lectures. But before we conclude this
setting-out of the problem, one question remains. At
an early point in this lecture, I have said that "traditional class struggles are no longer the dominant
expression of the unsociable sociability of man.
Instead we find more individual and more occasional
manifestations of social aggression. Violations of law
and order are prominent among them." What, one
may ask, does the problem of law and order have to
do with traditional class struggles? The answer is yet
another response to our question about the difference between riots and revolutions. It is above all the
framework in which our analysis seeks its place.

Man's unsociable sociability has many faces. Electoral and parliamentary conflict between political
parties which are based on the divergent interests of
social classes is but one of these faces, and arguably
the civilised exception. Looking down one side of the
spectrum of social aggression, we soon encounter
organised conflicts which are much less manageable.
The struggle between modern classes itself took
some time to be channelled into the ritual of adver-
sary politics. There are sectional, religious, regional
conflicts which seem all but incapable of solution;
Beirut and Belfast has been mentioned several
times. Rebellion, guerilla fighting, civil war all
belong in this vicinity. They are forms of demanding
change, which always means at least a place in the
sun for those in darkness, against more or less recal-

citrant authorities and those who benefit from them. As we go up the scale of intensity and violence of such conflicts, we encounter the familiar climax of revolution. Revolutions are of course no accidents. The intensity and violence of solidary conflicts increases as it becomes more difficult for new social forces to gain recognition. The eruptions which are intended to blow open the rigidities of an *ancien régime* take place when they have become inevitable, not when some bearded leader says so. They are also great frustrations. Not only does the eruption itself maim many, but its lava soon freezes into a social landscape which is hardly less rigid and usually less attractive than the one it replaced. The social contract is suspended for one ecstatic moment, only to be reinstated in its most unbearable Hobbesian form.

But the same social force of social aggression or unsociable sociability can also find expression in individual acts, and it is this observation which stands at the outset of our analysis. Moreover, solitary conflicts and individual actions are convertible into each other. Werner Sombart was the first to argue that there is no socialism in the United States because individuals can satisfy their desire for greater life chances by dreaming, and often living, the American dream.[56] Perhaps, social and geographical mobility are the individual equivalent, and often the concomitant, of civilised parliamentary debate. Often, individual acts are more destructive than what Marx, who disliked mobility, called disdainfully "competition between individuals."[57] Suicide is a prime example of self-destructiveness, though the slow suicide of addiction must today come a close second.

When destructiveness turns against others, it becomes crime, above all, violence against persons, the denial of property, the undermining of institutions.

Again, one might construct a scale of intensity and violence. One would then discover that the two ends of the spectrum are not very far from each other. Whereas civil war and revolution tear the fabric of the social contract apart, suicide and crime punch holes in it until in the end it cannot hold any more. Either way, in leaps and bounds or by stealth, we find ourselves on a road to Anomia. It is pointless to wonder which of these routes is worse. The former, class struggle right unto the edge of civil war and revolution, was the European social problem of the eighteenth and nineteenth centuries, beginning a little earlier in Britain and spilling over into our own century almost everywhere. The latter, the dissipation of law and order by impunity and the resulting disorder and uncertainty, is the social problem of our own time, and may well continue to be that for many decades to come. It needs to be understood before it can be contained, although it also needs to be contained unless we want to suffer the miseries of Anomia. Man's unsociable sociability is the key both to understanding and to containing the problem of law and order.

2. Seeking Rousseau, Finding Hobbes

In this lecture, I shall have to do something unpleasant, if not slightly distasteful, and attack my friends. For some considerable time, many of those who sought improvements in human life chances have been guided by an image of man which is as touching as it is unhelpful. They have assumed that if only people were freed of the constraints imposed on their actions by history, culture and society, they would live happily and peacefully ever after. Make people free to choose and they will behave in ways which are morally good and socially compliant! Increasingly, this notion has come to pervade views of education and leisure, but also programmes of political participation and criminal justice. It is a pleasing image; in important respects it may even be true, though this is something which we cannot know. But we can know that this image of man is one of the landmarks on the road to Anomia. This is what I propose to demonstrate, while wondering all the time what other image of man should take its place.

If one attacks one's friends, one is easily misunderstood. Let there be no doubt: the argument of this lecture is not that it was, or is wrong to free people from constraints and open up opportunities for choice. When Rousseau wrote that "man is born free, and yet he lies in chains", he had much to go on.[1] From the vantage point of the French and American revolutions, and even the so-called industrial revolution, improving life chances meant in the first instance, and in the second and third as well, increasing options. Man's "departure from his self-imposed infancy" (as Kant defined enlightenment[2]) involved of necessity breaks with unquestioned bonds. But history remains forever unfinished. The very dynamic of the unfolding of enlightenment created, from a certain point onwards, contradictions and new problems. Such new problems have a curious effect on people. Some will argue that the way to solve them is by doing more of the same. They close their eyes to the fact that today's problems are the result—economists would say, the spillovers or externalities—of yesterday's solutions. Doing more of the same may be worthy, but it is neither wise nor effective. Others suggest that because yesterday's solutions have created today's problems, we must undo these solutions and return to the previous state. But these advocates of a reversal of trends ignore that undoing yesterday's solutions will merely take us back to the problems of the day before. If history makes any sense, and if progress has meaning—of which admittedly we cannot be sure—this too is bad advice. In fact, we must go on to new horizons, following perhaps the course of the knight in chess by moving both sideways and forward.

Enlarging options for a growing number of people was one of the fundamental changes of history. It was, and is the process which can be called, modernity. The stages of the process are many, from the early and hesitant discovery of the individual in philosophical theory and constitutional practice, through the establishment of the principle of free contract to such benefits of modernity as mobility, participation, and a decent standard of living for most. Yet these massive increases in life chances and liberty had a price in predictability and order. This is not surprising. Liberty always tends towards anarchy, and we have seen that there may be a strain towards anomy in modern societies. But this strain is self-destructive. Anarchy and anomy do not strengthen liberty. On the contrary, when spillovers become larger than the main reservoir, and externalities can no longer be internalised, liberty is at risk. Somewhere, there is a threshold beyond which the cost of modernity begins to exceed its benefits.

The cost of increasing options involves first the normative structure of society. Freedom to choose means almost by definition the absence of normative constraints on our actions. In fact, the reduction of such constraints has been a long, complex, and many would say, incomplete process. Paradoxical though it may appear, the process began with the rule of law, that is the explication and generalisation of normative constraints. The law took the place of more pervasive traditional prescriptions and the absolute power that often went with them. Formalised law implies limitations which are absent from older and other types of normative structure. At a later stage, the limitation of constraints by legalisation was followed by the contraction of the law, and notably criminal law. We have described a part of this process when we referred to "no-go areas" which signify change, as in the case of abortion, homosexuality, adultery. Leon Radzinowicz makes the point that "the trend towards contraction has been confined to a very few countries which combine strong liberal traditions with a measure of basic stability," and that even in these countries there have more recently been "inexorable pressures towards expansion."[3] Legalisation has been followed by juridification, the rule of law by a plethora of laws, rules, and orders, and court judgments. However, this has hardly contributed to the effectiveness, or even the legitimacy of norms; it may well have done the reverse. In any case, the relaxation of normative constraints has reached a point at which it no longer promotes liberty. We are back to impunity, Anomia, and the consequences for society and the individual.

The tidal turn of modernity from a force for freedom to a force for uncertainty and anomy has been aggravated by a half-intended consequence of the extension of options. It was a matter of course that options should be gained at the expense of normative constraints, but in the process, they have also affected those firmer bonds which transcend short-term social changes and anchor people in the deeper stream of culture. We have called them, ligatures (though there may be other and better names).[4] Ligatures are cultural bonds associated with certain basic units to which individuals belong by virtue of forces outside their reach rather than by choice. They lead us into the world of familial ties, membership of society, religion, perhaps age group and gender, and on a less fundamental level, locality, vocation and class as well. One would associate such values as solidarity, but also authority, and faith with these bonds. All ligatures add a dimension of tradition, of living history, to the essentially contemporary quality of norms and sanctions. In any case, ligatures provide the basic certainty without which the normative structure of society could not be sustained, the moral dimension of legitimacy as well as the dimension of meaning for individual behaviour.

One of the fascinating aspects of the story of expanding options is how this process has made inroads into relationships which seemed immune from the universe of choice. Turning religion from an unquestioned bond into an optional extra was of course part and parcel of what we commonly call, enlightenment. With increasing mobility, local and general social bonds too became available rather than given. Vocations and trades have long been transformed into jobs for many. Secular marriage, easier divorce, greater rights for children and numerous other processes all the way to alternative forms of communal living have transformed family ties into temporary contracts. In the end, even the biologically based distinctions of age and sex are, as it were, put up for auction; in the United States, it is illegal to distinguish people by their age or gender for purposes of employment and social position, and even the German Christian Democrats decided at a Party

Conference that men and women must to all intents
and purposes be "interchangeable." The optional
world which emerges as a result of such trends has
increased the freedom of Catholics or Germans, car-
penters or aristocrats, wives or children to be something different. But it has also raised a curious set of
new questions. Why should it be desirable to be different if difference itself is abolished? What do
choices mean if everything becomes equally valid?

Even without invoking the nausea of existentialist
thinking on this matter—and the *acte gratuite* which
responds, and which might well take the form of
suicide or crime[5]—it is clear that a world with
severely weakened ligatures is a disorienting and dis-
concerting world. Solidarity, authority, faith, and a
sense of history are not easily replaced. If the contraction of the normative structure of society goes
hand in hand with the destruction of cultural bonds,
we get dangerously close not only to Anomia, but to
the most brutal imagery of a state of nature. And all
this is from one point of view the result—the unintended but apparently inevitable result—of an image
of man which has guided the process.

This image has left its traces all over, but in our context its application to criminal justice is most telling.
Werner Maihofer, one of the spokesmen of the
"alternative professors" who designed and promoted
the reform of criminal law in Germany, himself argues
that "nothing is as crucial for the style of an age of law"
as "the notion of man which it employs as its point of
orientation." Indeed, criminal law reform "is ultimately about nothing other than the 'image of man'
which its authors presuppose."[6] Criminal law reform

involves the replacement of one such image by another.

Maihofer begins by attacking the notion that man is a free moral personality, capable of discriminating between good and evil. This Kantian notion over- looks the fundamental fact that apart from physical there are social constraints on our decisions and actions. A " 'modern image' of man" must get away from the "abstract subject" of the "isolated individ- ual" and take into account man's "sociality," the fact that he always acts "as someone," as a poor, deprived, black, young slumdweller for example.[7]

This notion of man "as a 'socialised being' " has obvious consequences for the related questions of responsibility and punishment. Today, responsibility too is individualised. But conscience and moral judg- ments are a product of society. Thus "the socially inadequate behaviour of a person cannot just have the reason that this person has failed although he would have had the capacity to behave 'correctly' (adequately), but the reason must also lie equally more or less exclusively with society: 'the others'."[8] It is therefore necessary to find out whether offenders were ever in a position to absorb "socially adequate" distinctions between good and evil. They must not be held responsible for acts to which they were driven by force of circumstance.

In terms of punishment, this notion of man as a "socialised being" means that all penalties which effectively "de-socialise" people are questionable. This is notably true for all forms of detention, because the "counter-society" in which prison inmates find themselves serves their "asocialisation"

or "antisocialisation" rather than "resocialisation."
Maihofer quotes Franz von List at this point: "If a
young person or even an adult has committed a
crime and we let him go, the probability that he
will commit another crime is lower than if we
punish him." What then is the purpose of punishment? "To prevent people from asocial or anti-
social behaviour by threatening punishment for
certain unbearable violations of the law and if
despite that they transgress the boundaries which
the law is designed to protect by 'crime', to make
possible future social behaviour by imposing punishment."[9]

This means of course that detention must be the
rare exception rather than the rule. In the normal
course of events, the criminal needs care not punishment; indeed "punishment [is] the *ultima ratio* of
social policy." This leads Maihofer to a casuistry of
delinquents and penalties: occasional offenders who
are ready to repent should not be imprisoned even
for serious crimes; occasional offenders who are
unrepentant should be punished but by fines and
socially useful work rather than imprisonment; persistent offenders who are capable of improvement
should receive "educational punishment" to
resocialise them; recidivists who are incapable of
improvement should be punished by a dignified form
of detention in order to guarantee their security and
that of society. "The ultimate failure of the criminal
is often more fate than guilt."[10]

Maihofer ends this paper which was written in
1964 with a flourish. He invokes "the 'social age of
law' of socialised man", in which punishment as the

imposition of evil for evil will not 'die out', but in which it will as far as possible become an invitation and instigation to balance evil with good, whereby alone in our contemporary understanding a justice on earth can be practised which transforms this world not into a worse, but into a better place."[11]

It is easy to see the effect of such theories, though it is little less easy to detect the flaw in their reasoning. The effect, intended by their authors—and Maihofer is but one of many who could be cited to this effect[12]—is precisely that weakening of sanctions to the point of impunity which we have described as the real problem of law and order. We shall return to the flaws of reasoning presently. But first, one amendment or addition is necessary. Maihofer argues that the image of man as the autonomous person capable of discriminating between good and evil has to be replaced by that of "socialised man," that is man the product of forces outside his control. In fact however, this is not what he proposes at all. "Socialised man" is for him merely an instrument for the exculpation of the perpetrators of criminal acts. The image of man underlying this operation is one of beings who are essentially good. Whatever they do wrong is the fault of forces over which they have no control and which are largely social in character. Left to their own resources, their behaviour would not only be "socially adequate" but also morally acceptable. The purpose of criminal justice is to contribute to bringing about that "better world" in which more people are left to their own resources in this sense, that is allowed to be their good selves.

This view should not be dismissed too easily as

naïve. There may be naïve versions of it among lawyers as well as educationists, but there are also highly
subtle versions. Indeed, we are setting foot here on
the territory of one of the great social thinkers of our
time, Jürgen Habermas. Habermas is the heir of the
so-called Frankfurt School. Despite his unusual
sophistication, he has thus never abandoned some of
the egg shells of Hegel, including the temptation to
lock himself into the mechanics of dialectical thinking. So far as the fundamental problem of social
order is concerned, the pre-modern answer was non-
rational, almost instinctual. It consisted in the
acceptance of living bonds which were given validity
by the "aura of the sacred" and an "image of the
world" which was the "product of a synthesizing
imagination."[13] The second phase, modernity,
means above all legalisation. Hobbes wins, as it
were. "The self-consciousness of this phase has
found its most consistent expression in Hobbes'
Leviathan. This is interesting in our context in so far
as Hobbes constructs the social order exclusively
from the system perspective of the state which con-
stitutes civil society."[14] Like Hegel, Marx, and the
Frankfurt "critical theorists," Habermas spends
much time on the detailed description of this condition which they all pursue with a frisson of fascina-
tion in disgust. As a result, much less time is spent on
the future for which civil and bourgeois society is
merely the prelude, and which offers a synthesis of
the two earlier models of social order; yet this is the
keystone of the whole edifice of ideas.

In one crucial respect we can follow Habermas
unreservedly. He too states that minds part company

over the question of "whether they hold on to the intentions of enlightenment, however broken they may be, or whether they abandon the project of modernity as lost."[15] Habermas's project is not a denial of "system integration," that is of the normative structure of civil society. Yet unquestionably he sees this as a mere shell within which real life, what he calls the *Lebenswelt*, the "life world" can flourish. He defines this world in many ways, though the common feature of these attempts is that it is "a network of co-operation by the medium of communication."[16]

> "What ties the socialised individuals to each other and secures the integration of society, is a web of communicative actions which can succeed only in the light of cultural traditions—and not systemic mechanisms which are removed from the intuitive understanding of its members. The life world which members construct from common cultural traditions, is co-extensive with society. It draws all social processes into the searchlight of cooperative efforts at interpretation. It lends everything that happens in society the transparency of something that can be talked about—even if one does not (yet) understand it."[17];

The key idea is clear despite the language which Habermas has chosen; the idea recurs throughout his great work on communicative action and was present in many of his earlier writings. Civil and bourgeois society has opened up spaces for a kind of social order which does not have to be based primarily on norms enforced by sanctions and backed up by institutionalised power. Instead, "normatively united communicative action" can step in,[18] a world of "free discourse," including "theoretical discourses in science and scholarship, moral and practical discourses in the political public and the legal system, finally aesthetic criticism in art and literature."[19] "Can complex societies have a rational identity?" Habermas asked in earlier writings. His optimistic reply takes one to the heart of his beliefs: "Only the communicative ethic secures the generality of admissible norms and the autonomy of actors by the chance of the discursive realisation of claims to validity with which norms appear, that is by those and only those norms being able to claim validity on which all concerned agree, or would agree (without force) as participants of a discourse, once they enter, or would enter into a discursive process of forming a will."[20] Or again: "The appropriate model is the community of communication of all concerned who as participants in a practical discourse examine the claim of norms to validity, and insofar as they accept it with reasons, reach the conviction that under given circumstances norms are 'right'."[21] In other words, the validity of norms does not rest on sanctions and power, but on the consensus of those affected which is reached by rational debate and on the strength of plausible reasons.

This is Rousseau. "If one frees," Rousseau says, "the social contract of all inessentials, one will find that it can be reduced to the following formula: each of us places his person and his whole strength under the direction of the general will; we accept every member into a body as an inseparable part of the whole."[22] It is moreover Rousseau rather than Hegel. Hegel had unfriendly things to say about Rousseau's "general will," because this is merely the community of individual wills, and society thus only the result of a contract, when in reality (in Hegel's reality) an "objective will" determines what must be whether individuals like it or not.[23] In this sense at least, Rousseau is the democrat and Hegel the authoritarian, and Habermas has chosen the side of Rousseau. When he says, rational, he is thinking of a process of reasoning rather than the goddess of reason.

Habermas is Rousseau in another, deeper sense as well. Once again, we encounter a telling image of man. It is that of natural goodness and social deformation, and thus of the need to de-socialise "socialised man" in order to bring out his good nature; it is Émile. It is useful to remind oneself of his story as one wonders which image of man serves a free society best.

Émile of course is Rousseau's brainchild.[24] It helps that he is not only an orphan, but also a "Wasp," certainly white, if not Anglo-Saxon then pure French, Protestant in a manner of speaking, healthy, wealthy and physically strong. (Rousseau does not seem to have noticed that the very conditions which he builds into Émile's anti-authoritarian education invalidate some of his conclusions.) From the outset, Émile's education is totally free. Far from being designed to "socialise" him, the very last things he is taught are the rules and roles of society. "The only habit that the child should be allowed to contract is that of having no habits; let him be carried on either arm, let him be accustomed to offer either hand, to use one or other indifferently; let him not want to eat, sleep, or do anything at fixed hours, nor be unable to be left alone by day or night."[25] Émile is not exposed to the painful tests of the Protestant ethic, or as sociologists would have it, to deferred gratification, to "that cruel condition which sacrifices the present to an uncertain future, that burdens a child with all sorts of restrictions and begins by making him miserable, in order to prepare him for some far-off happiness which he may never enjoy"; no, he gets "the delights of liberty" right away.[26] They mean, among other things, that "the very words *obey* and *command* will be excluded from his vocabulary, still more those of *duty* and *obligation*."[27] This is possible only because the teacher exercises his authority by letting the child be in charge. Thus a young man grows up who is really free. "He does not know the meaning of habit, routine, and custom; what he did yesterday has no control over what he is doing today; he follows no rule, submits to no authority, copies no pattern, and only acts or speaks as he pleases."[28]

But of course, Émile grows up. While the hermit may be most autonomous, and even happiest, he is not self-sufficient. Robinson is but the first lesson, and perhaps not a very good one at that. "Man's weakness makes him sociable."[29] This means that society is above all there to help the weak. It is a society of equals, until and unless someone needs the help of others. Pity on them is the first maxim of social manners. The civil order which gradually emerges from the happier state of nature is less humane; it is governed by "those specious words—justice and subordination."[30] Thus at 18, Émile realises that all the world's a stage; indeed, worse than that, "he will grieve to see his brothers tearing each other limb from limb for a mere dream, and transforming themselves into wild beasts because they could not be content to be men."[31] So, "how can a young man take part in the business of life?"[32] The answer, not surprisingly, is to rely on nature rather than men. Émile, at any rate, "is a man of nature's making, not man's."[33]

What, then, about his ligatures? Rousseau takes great pains to make sure that even religion is discovered by Émile himself. It is not simply accepted because it is given. Indeed, the Savoyard Priest tells a long tale about "natural religion," the incomprehensibility of most things transcendent, of eternity, morality, and the rest. Perhaps, man does not need religion at all: "Oh, let us have man unspoilt; he will always find it easy to be good and he will always be happy without remorse."[34] But given the fact that there are religions, one may as well "respect all religions, and [get] each to live peaceably in his own religion."[35] Thus, freedom does extend to the world of ligatures as well, to religion, and even to morality. "But moral duties have their modifications, their exceptions, their rules. When human weakness makes an alternative inevitable, of two evils choose the least; in any case it is better to commit a misdeed than to contract a vicious habit."[36]

Not that Émile commits many misdeeds; obeying the "laws of nature" first, he is respectful, modest, humble, quiet, soft-spoken, tender, sensitive, in short, a really nice young man, who duly informs his master about the theories of education which he has imbibed:

> "I have decided to be what you made me; of my own free will I will add no fetters to those imposed upon me by nature and the laws. The more I study the works of men in their institutions, the more clearly I see that, in their efforts after independence, they become slaves, and that their very freedom is wasted in vain attempts to assure its continuance. That they may not be carried away by the flood of things, they form all sorts of attachments; then as soon as they wish to move forward they are surprised to find that everything drags them back. It seems to me that to set oneself free we need do nothing, we need only continue to desire freedom."[37]

But on closer inspection, things are not quite as simple as that. Not only does Émile continue his reply with the suspiciously Hegelian statement, "my master, you have made me free by teaching me to yield to necessity," there is above all Sophy who does not seem to fit in the natural order of things. She is no doubt a nice girl, but very much an unliberated woman. "Needlework is what Sophy likes best."[38] Fortunately, she comes from the right kind of family; for a man must never marry above his station. "As the family is only connected with society through its head, it is the rank of that head which decides that of the family as a whole."[39] Undoubtedly, this social gradient makes the relation between Émile and Sophy proper in other respects as well. Says the

master to Sophy: "When Émile became your hus-
band, he became your head; it is yours to obey; this
is the will of nature."[40] Our modern Rousseaueans
would not like such distinctions much. They would
be quick to point out that there is something dis-
tinctly cultural, not to say dated, about Rousseau's
notion of nature. But they might join forces with him
again when he concludes: "Thus the age of reason
becomes for the one the age of licence; for the other,
the age of reasoning."[41]

There is no shortage of familiar topics in Émile's
story. One need not go to Dr. Spock or to Summer-
hill to find it applied. It underlies a long history of
practical changes from the Declaration of the Rights
of Man and Citizen in 1789 to criminal law reform in
Europe in the 1960s. Indeed, this is one of the points
to be made about Rousseau, that under conditions of
traditional authoritarianism his image of man and
society is a prescription for radical reform in the
interest of advancing liberty. It is therefore no accident that Rousseau became the hero of the two great
revolutions of modernity, nor that he has remained
the hero of those whose main concern is with the
heavy hand of traditional authority.

But taken out of this context, the imagery looks
very different. In one sense, the story of Émile is that
of the hermit, the recluse, the non-social being. All
that is society is not only polluted but polluting. If
this is not the theory of "retreatism," it is that of
"rebellion."[42] It would serve Max Stirner's "singular
one" well who puts his own thing above all others.[43]
Thus James Joll has an important point when he
says: "The fundamental idea that man is by nature

good and that it is institutions which corrupt him remains the basis of all anarchist thought. . . . And, just as in Émile's ideal education, the child's latent qualities are drawn out by sincerity, simplicity, liberty and natural behaviour, so in the anarchist society men's instincts for good will be brought out by much the same treatment."[44]

But this is precisely where suspicions arise. J. L. Talmon has voiced them in their extreme form when he described Rousseau as the true author of "totalitarian democracy."[45] The general will applied, Talmon argued, must mean the imposition of a usurper's will on the uninterested and on the unwilling too. Talmon looked for psychological roots of Rousseau's aberrations. He was "obsessed with the idea of man's cupidity as the root cause of moral degeneration and social evil"; he belonged to those who "either out of a sense of guilt or out of weariness, long to be delivered from the need for external recognition and the challenge of rivalry."[46] There is indeed a world between these obsessions and Adam Smith's, or Kant's confident acceptance of "cupidity" and "rivalry" as motive forces of progress and liberty.

However, we can do without a psychoanalysis of Jean-Jacques Rousseau to appreciate what the application of his image of man and society would mean. It is not totalitarian, to be sure, any more than Sartre's notion of gratuitous acts in a moral void makes him an ideologist of fascism.[47] But it is a prescription not only for anarchy, but for anomy as well, and insofar as anomy is a condition in which the ugly weed of totalitarian rule sprouts, there is a relation.

Let us imagine a society of Émiles, or even a community of reasonable communication *à la* Habermas. What if someone, just one, Emil or Emilio, does not play the game? The others talk to him, they reason with him. But he will not listen. He continues to disturb the peace either by open dissent, or sneaking deviance, by crime. He has to be isolated, expelled from the community, one against the general will. What if it is two, or twenty? Even one is enough to destroy the beauty of an idea which lives and dies by its perfection. And of course, when the general will turns into the tyranny of the majority it is much worse than the rule of law which it has replaced; there is no recourse against such tyranny. Digging a little deeper, there clearly are not only obstreperous individuals, but divergent interests by entire categories of people. What if "unconstrained communication" leads nowhere in a dispute between employers and workers about wages or hours of work? What of the intractable battles between religious, regional ethnic groups? One does not need to go on to discover the simple truth of the refrain in Brecht's *Threepenny Opera*, "but circumstances aren't like that."[48] Circumstances show sufficient evidence of the contrariness of human nature.

This in turn means that to the extent to which the normative structure of society is suspended, and notably if sanctions are left to allegedly self-governing communities unconstrained by powers external to them, turmoil ensues. It is no good arguing that this would be just a transitional stage until the education of man is complete *C'est le provisoire qui dure*. Nothing lasts longer than the transitional. All those whose search for Rousseau has not remained confined to the fight against an *ancien régime*, should bear in mind the possibility that as they succeed, they may well encounter a very different world from that of Émile, because:

" . . . in the nature of man, we find three principal causes of quarrel. First, competition; secondly, diffidence; thirdly, glory.

The first, makes men invade for gain; the second, for safety; and the third, for reputation. The first use violence, to make themselves masters of other men's persons, wives, children, and cattle; the second, to defend them; the third, for trifles, as a word, a smile, a different opinion, and any other signs of undervalue, either direct in their persons, or by reflection in their kindred, their friends, their nation, their profession, or their name.

Hereby it is manifest, that during the time men live without a common power to keep them all in awe, they are in that condition which is called war; and such a war, as is of every man, against every man. . . .

Whatsoever therefore is consequent to a time of war, where every man is enemy to every man; the same is consequent to a time, wherein men live without other security than what their own strength and their own invention shall furnish them withall. In such condition, there is no place for industry; because the fruit thereof is uncertain; and consequently no culture of the earth, no navigation, nor use of the commodities that may be imported by sea; no commodious building; no instruments of moving, and removing such things as require much force; no knowledge of the face of the earth; no account of time; no arts; no letters; no society; and which is worst of all, continual fear, and danger of violent death; and the life of man, solitary, poor, nasty, brutish, and short."[49]

This may not be a description of Harlem or the Bronx, Brixton or Toxteth, if only because these are islands of Hobbes in a sea of fairly ordered prosperity. Yet—to take issue with one more friend—the advice given by some in the face of spreading disorder will lead us further into the quagmire rather than out of it. It is clearly useful to have an accountable police force and more community policing as well as a liberal (whatever that is) handling of the law. However, to be guided by an image of "order without law" is but another search for Rousseau which will end with Hobbes. It is indeed no surprise to find, in this context, the statement "that a society which makes gods out of economics, production, competition and the Gross National Product, while paying insufficient attention to the creation of those human values which represent the quality of the social order, will always require more police, bigger prisons, and will generate a boom in the sale of locks, bolts and bars."[50] "Cupidity" and "rivalry" as the enemies again! And not surprisingly, applied Habermas in the end: "Throughout my experience in the police forces of England, I have continually been impressed by the level of potential for a more orderly, happy and just society. I can think of no better way to provide for the full realization of this potential than by fashioning a communitarian movement as the basis of social order."[51]

In fact, Habermas is more cautious, or perhaps he has simply thought more about about the subject. He does not deny the observer's approach to social order as a normative system, much as he prefers the participant's experience of the life world. However, this dual perspective is no way out of the dilemma. So where do we go from here? Having been so rough with a number of friends, it is probably consistent to seek a first reply with someone whose conservative inclinations have led him and others around him astray when it mattered. Arnold Gehlen defends institutions like the law, the family, and property precisely because they are not natural. They are cultural achievements, and as such precarious. If we take them away, man becomes more natural perhaps, but this means more primitive and unstable. "I take precisely the reverse point of view from the 18th century," says Gehlen. "It is time for a Counter-Rousseau, for a philosophy of pessimism and of the seriousness of life. 'Back to nature' means for Rousseau: culture disfigures man, the state of nature shows him in full naïveté, justice and animation. Against that and conversely, it seems to us today that the state of nature in man is chaos, is the head of Medusa at the sight of which one is paralysed." Culture, law, morality, discipline need to be defended at a time at which "the law becomes elastic, art nervous, and religion sentimental. The experienced eye begins to see under the froth, the head of Medusa, man becomes *natural* and everything becomes possible. The order of the day must be: back to culture!

For the road forward evidently leads with quick steps towards nature since the progress of civilisation has demonstrated to us the full weakness of human nature unprotected by strict forms."[52]

Gehlen's analysis is clearly pertinent. But are the Counter-Rousseaus merely to be found in Hobbes a century-and-a-half before, or in Arnold Gehlen a century-and-a-half after the *Contrat Social*? And why should the road *forward* be an inexorable journey to natural disaster whereas we are free to go *back* to culture? Fortunately, the fertile eighteenth century holds answers to both these questions. We do not need Rousseau to guide us, nor do we need Hobbes, or Gehlen for that matter, to help us avoid his fallacies. Six years after Rousseau's death, in 1784, Immanuel Kant published the piece entitled, "Idea for a General History With Cosmopolitan Intent."[53] On less than 20 pages, it makes more sense so far as images of man and society are concerned than volumes of philosophical anthropology. Since we have used Kant's terminology already, and will go on doing so, we may as well make sure that it is placed in its proper context.

Kant begins his argument in characteristic critical spirit. We do not know whether history has any meaning. "History has no meaning," Karl Popper would say a century-and-a-half later, only to add in true Kantian spirit: "Although history has no meaning, we can give it meaning."[54] If there is any "natural intention" in the history of man, Kant himself said, it must surely be the development of man's capacities by his own efforts. This takes Kant to the two key points of his argument: in order to bring about the unfolding of man's capacities, nature has provided him with unique means; and man is in a position to devise a method for making this natural potential of progress real.

First then, nature, and Kant's image of man. The means by which man develops his capacities is "their antagonism within society, insofar as this becomes in the end the cause of a lawful order."[55] In other words, conflict is the creative force of history once it is not allowed to roam freely as a war of all against all, but is domesticated. "I understand by this antagonism the unsociable sociability of man, that is their inclination to enter into society which is yet combined with a pervasive resistance that permanently threatens to divide society." Kant has remarkable things to say about this "unsociable sociability" which display a very different confidence in man's "cupidity" and the attitude to "rivalry" between people which are so abhorred by Rousseau. It is in fact the antagonism of the desire to socialise and the other desire to remain singular which produces the resistance by which alone man can overcome his innate laziness and strive to find a place among others, driven by "the search for honour, for power, and for property." Thus, it is a good thing that we cannot suffer our fellow-men, but cannot live without them either:

> "Without those not very amiable qualities of unsociability which give rise to the resistance which everyone encounters of necessity in his selfish arrogations, all talents would forever remain in their buds in an Arcadian shepherd's life of complete harmony, self-sufficiency and

mutual love: men, good-natured like the sheep on their pastures, would give their existence no greater value than their cattle has; they would not fill the void of creation in regard of its purpose, as rational nature. Thanks be therefore to nature for the quarrelsomeness, for the mischievously competitive vanity, for the insatiable lust to have and also to rule! Without it all splendid natural talents would slumber forever undeveloped in mankind. Man wants harmony; but nature knows better what is good for its kind; it wants conflict."

This leads Kant to his second major point, the need to set up a "civil society" which "generally administers the law."[56] Kant shares Hobbes's view (and that of others) that it is need and necessity which enforce the social contract. What people tend to do to each other makes it impossible for them to live together in "wild freedom"; it is necessary to define the boundaries of freedom precisely, and to secure them. "Liberty under external laws combined to the greatest extent with irresistible force" is thus the task of self-domestication both nationally and internationally. But this must not, and cannot blunt the force of human progress. "All culture and art, those ornaments of mankind, the most beautiful social order are fruits of that unsociability which has to discipline itself and thus develop the seedcorn of nature completely by the efforts of culture."

Kant's image of man, and of the social contract were not new at the time. Rather amusingly, the author of the article on Hobbes in the great *Encyclopédie*, contrasts "the philosopher from Malmesbury"

with "the philosopher from Geneva": "The philosophy of M. Rousseau of Geneva is almost the
reverse of that of Hobbes. One believes that man is
by nature good, the other that he is evil. . . . It is
laws and the formation of society which have
improved men, if one follows Hobbes: and which
have depraved him, if one follows M.Rousseau." In
fact, the author adds, a third approach is the right
one; the "perpetual vicissitudes" of the human condition are due to the fact that man is both good and
bad.[57] Even before the *encyclopédistes*, David
Hume, to whom Kant owed so much, advanced his
own notion of the unsociable sociability of man. We
need society not only because of our "infirmity" and
the resulting "necessities", but "there are other par-
ticulars in our natural temper, and in our outward
circumstances, which are very incommodious, and
even contrary to the requisite conjunction", among
them above all "our selfishness."[58] Men are not just
selfish; they may even on balance be more kind than
self-centred; but both motives compete. John Locke
before him took it for granted that whatever sociable
motives men may have, the threat of a "state of war"
is a powerful incentive for men "putting themselves
into society and quitting the state of nature."[59] And
as we go forward from Kant to the present, we are
back with Karl Popper's eloquent plea for progress:
"For those who have eaten from the tree of knowledge, paradise is lost. The more we try to return to
the heroic age of tribalism, the more surely do we
arrive at the Inquisition, at the Secret Police, and at
a romanticised gangsterism. Beginning with suppression of reason and truth, we must end with the most

brutal and violent destruction of all that is human. There is no return to a harmonious state of nature. If we turn back, then we must go the whole way—we must return to the beasts."[60]

It is good to be in distinguished company, but it is better to be right, or rather to know why one takes a certain position. The question is not what human nature really is; such essentialist speculation is far from our approach. Of course, the observed behaviour of people is relevant. It is risky to assume human beings who are unlike anyone who has ever been seen. In terms of our everyday experience, the least that can be said about Kant's notion of the unsociable sociability of man is that it makes sense. But the more important question in our context is, what kind of image of man—and society—is most likely to take us to an understanding of liberty, law and order which is persuasive and allows of practical applications which do not refute it. I suggest that it is an image which leads to the concept of the social contract as the domestications of man's unsociable sociability in the interest of progress, that is of the forever unfinished process of increasing our life chances by our own efforts.

Precisely this social contract appears to be at risk. It is always at risk; the great social force which Kant calls, "antagonism," fortunately never dies. The whole point about cultivating conflict by the creation of institutions is that conflict remains alive as a creative force of improvement. But in some contemporary societies, the risk for the social contract is unusually great. This is what the problem of law and order tells us. This is why impunity, and the loosening of ligatures, are so serious.

What then is the flaw in Werner Maihofer's argument about crime and punishment? We have held up Kant against this contemporary critic who has in fact written a little book trying to refute Kant's "Idea for a General History With Cosmopolitan Intent."[61] Maihofer's insistence that man can be himself only as a member of society is a recipe for relativism in theory, and conformism in practice. Its pragmatic implication that man is by nature good is also unhelpful as an argument for freedom. But these may be called debating points. The flaw in his argument about the responsibilities of "socialised man" is a different one, and it is important. Maihofer argues that crime is essentially the fault of society, and that the remedy which must therefore take the place of traditional punishment is a matter for social policy. Others have followed him in this line of reasoning[62]; indeed it may be said to underly much of recent criminal law reform.

What happens in this argument is a fascinating, but highly explosive confusion of law and social policy or, as we shall prefer to say, of law and economics. If the notion of law is to make any sense at all, it refers to rules which apply absolutely. Either certain forms of behaviour are ruled out as contrary to the law, and are therefore sanctioned, or not. Ruling them out may be accompanied by all sorts of "ifs" and even "whens," but at the end of the day the question is whether a given act or set of actions is such as to contravene the law or not. This again may be hard to discover. There is often a temptation to say that to some extent a breach of the law has occurred, whereas in other respects a given set of actions is compatible with the law. But such reservations do not detract from the absolute or, if one does not like the word, the unambiguous quality of the law. There are good reasons for the ancient principle, *iudex non calculat*.

On the other hand, *oeconomicus semper calculat*. Economics as the science (or, if you prefer, the art) of scarcity is invariably about more or less, about quantities and relationships. This has probably something to do with economic laws, a question which we shall leave on one side in our context. All that matters here is that there is one approach to what people do which asks whether it is right or wrong, and another approach which asks how little or how much of it is appropriate for certain purposes. This also means that there are certain actions which lead us into the sphere of crime and punishment, and others which require economic (and social) policy.

Confusion of the two is widespread in the modern world; it is also tempting, and what is more, it is not at all easy to unravel. One kind of confusion arises when issues which appear to belong in the sphere of economics are redefined as issues of law. Two topical examples are the attempts to establish a "right to work" and a "right to a clean environment." The frequent assertion that poverty, whether in our own countries or in the developing world, is a "violation of human rights" belongs in the same category. In all these cases, it is easy to detect legal issues, as when emissions from factory chimneys are proved to cause skin diseases or worse, or if workers are sacked in contravention of employment protection laws. But this is not what is meant. Indeed the very purpose of the claims is to remove certain issues from the (relative) sphere of economics to the (absolute) sphere of the law. Yet it can probably be shown that they do not belong there. It is only by economic and social action that the underlying problems can be dealt with. No court of law can abolish unemployment or poverty.

The other confusion is that which delivers the law to economics. It has many forms. In the United States, negotiable penalties ("plea bargaining") have become the rule rather than the exception, and Europe is not immune to such developments. Discretion in the application of the law has at all levels become a balancing of incompatible factors, as when the police, or the courts, consider that because a man is unemployed one must be lenient about the theft which he has committed. The Maihofer approach— or should one say: the prevailing approach—turns such practice into a new principle. The principle is that however absolute the prescriptions, and above all proscriptions of the law may be, the sanctions associated with them belong properly into the sphere of economics. "Restrictions of the standard of living instead of short-term detention" is the title of one book on the subject.[63] However, the economic approach to sanctions removes their normative character, establishes impunity as desirable, and thereby destroys the normative structure of society.

Law and economics are both somewhat imperialist branches of human endeavour. Some lawyers take the stricture that they should not calculate to the extreme of believing that calculations are bad in principle, and that all human behaviour should be regulated by norms. Some economists imply, on the other hand, that all human behaviour can be explained by the competition for scarcity, and that the "invisible hand" will unfailingly see to it that the outcome of such competition is beneficial for all. Both are wrong. There is no market without the social contract, though if this contract turns into a jungle of laws and rules, man's unsociable sociability will be stifled and progress stopped. But the balance of market and norms remains a most difficult issue. For the student of liberty, the boundary between the two is crucial.

This is not the only question which must remain open in this brief comment on an ancient topic of legal, social and political thought.[64] But our intention was limited. It was to demonstrate a flaw in modern approaches to criminal justice, and to raise a precise question. The flaw is the economic fallacy in prevailing notions of the law. If one delivers sanctions to the sphere of economic and social policy, one not only accepts but actually promotes the invalidation of norms and therefore, Anomia. If this is so, the question can be put: how can the proper sphere of the law be defined for a free society? What is the role of sanctions in relation not only to law, but to liberty?

These are not just questions of theory. They have a direct bearing on political practice, and contemporary social structures have a direct bearing on them. We shall have to inspect these structures before we can hope to answer the question in the last of these lectures. But there is one other question to which we shall have to leave the answer open even at the end. We have seen that there are two forces which drive societies along the road to Anomia, or more appropriately, two kinds of vacuum which suck them down this road, One is impunity, the declining validity of social norms. The other is the progressive weakening of ligatures. It would be wrong to leave the social contract without at least wondering what might, and what does happen in this respect. Are there any signs of the reconstitution of those bonds without which the social contract cannot work?

The signs which there are probably tell us more about the problem than about its solution. The search for ligatures is a fashion, if not a force of our time; but more often than not, it leads people to embrace what can only be called, pseudo-ligatures, deceptive bonds which lead to frustration and sometimes destruction rather than confidence and reassurance.

Several authors have noted what both Daniel Bell and Philip Rieff have called, "the return of the sacred."[65] Some unlikely people—critical theorists like Erich Fromm and Max Horkheimer—have had this phenomenon visit upon themselves in their later years. At least one author, Hans Küng, has written important books trying to reconcile modern man with Christianity and thus reconstitute one important set of ligatures.[66] Küng's starting point is familiar to us: "The characteristic neurosis of our time is no longer the repression of sexuality and guilt, but disorientation, normlessness, lack of significance, of meaning, emptiness, and thus the repression of morality and religiosity."[67] Küng then tries to free (Catholic) Christianity of its anti-modern stance. He takes his readers right through the works of Marx and Nietzsche and Freud up to the point where they are faced with the "fundamental option" (as he characteristically says[68]) between trust and distrust, confidence and diffidence with regard to reality. Having opted for confidence, he believes, we must also opt for God, and having chosen God, for Christ.

Küng may have confirmed many in their faith, and persuaded some, though there are those who "can live without being confronted at all with Küng's fundamental option."[69] But above all, he demands a decision, and while he takes a hard route towards it, and from it, there are many who would prefer to have their ligatures more easily. The flourishing of quasi- and pseudo-religious sects is an indication. Some of these new creeds offer little and demand all. It is hard to forget the horrible picture of the "Reverend" Jones taking 918 men, women and children with him into his outsize suicide in Guyana. The event had a wider significance. Jean Baechler has convincingly described it in terms which suggest a striking parallel to Hitler resolving his gigantic personal problem by taking his people with him to death.[70]

At a lesser level, most attempts to reconstitute ligatures are fraught with dangers even as they offer new opportunities of meaning. Take decentralisation. When Fritz Schumacher gave his book the title, *Small Is Beautiful*, he caught the mood of the time. More than that, he actually set out to remedy symptoms which he himself listed as "crime, drug addiction, vandalism, mental breakdown, rebellion, and so forth," that is, the "human substance" of life.[71] His remedy was of course, smaller, more "appropriate" units of production and organisation. Since then, there has been a growing awareness of regional belonging in most parts of the modern world, a revival of ethnicity even in the United States, an insistence on a stronger voice for local interests everywhere, and a perceptible "communitarian movement" (to use a term which we have already encountered in connection with fighting crime).[72]

There is much that is clearly desirable about this trend. As much decentralisation as possible, as much centralisation as necessary, is a time-honoured liberal principle. But it has two sides; and while the burden of proof should be with those who want to remove decisions from where people actually live and work, many of the benefits of the modern world would disappear if decentralisation involved a return to nationalism, parochialism or even a war of all regions against all centres. More that that, strengthening local communities must not mean that the state, and the norms upheld by general and formal sanctions, are abandoned in favour of an unworkable Rousseauean mutuality or, more likely, an intolerable Hobbesian system of vigilantes exercising private power.

In a mobile society, the ligatures of locality are probably especially hard to re-establish. It is all the more important to pay attention to the search for new forms of solidarity in small groups the composition of which may change from time to time, but which provide a home for the homeless, bonds without which many, particularly among the young, could not live. So-called "alternative life styles" are, of course, far from general; they may even be a passing fad; but for a generation at least, life in "communes" of one kind or another has been a substitute for non-existent traditional families. On another level, it is characteristically the political left which advocates the strengthening of "small social networks" instead of bureaucratised social work to look after those who have been forgotten by the affluent society. Johano Strasser argues that we create social problems by the "bureaucratic-economic" way we define them. Neither capitalism nor really existing socialism can bring about the new order of human life in society which is necessary and which includes "alternative, communiterian forms of social security."[73] These have to be created "from below," by "democratisation" and "participation" in small units.

Such new solidarity too has much to recommend it, but is ambivalent like the other *ersatz* ligatures which we have mentioned. We are back with Habermas and his ideal communities of communication. Habermas is aware of their limitations as instruments of social policy,[74] and also of the other perspective of "system integration" and the rule of law. But others are not. Members and close sympathisers of the Baader-Meinhof group of terrorists have repeatedly emphasised the importance of being members of the group for their actions; belonging for them took precedence over morality. This is true for criminal gangs more generally, and the boundary between alternative and anti-system networks is not always clear.

One other observation provides an important case in point. Since the early 1970s a growing number of authors have exposed the contradictions of modernity in stark colours, only to conclude that what we need to resolve them is a "new social ethic." This was clearly implicit in the first Report to the Club of Rome, and has since become explicit in a further report concerned with communication. Here as elsewhere, communication has become a fashionable, unsentimental word for love and solidarity. Fritz Schumacher's book is not only about small units, but also about living with nature, and with others, rather than with things. Ed Mishan contributes to "the economic growth debate" his unending dream of a society without music records and cars, but with altruism and love. Fred Hirsch is more cautious, but leaves no doubt that only an ethic of solidarity can overcome the frustrations of positional competition. Lester Brown's "sustainable society" requires that we abandon the values of self-interest and gratification in favour of an ethics of common purpose. Erhard Eppler believes that the only way out of danger is a "change of consciousness" away from growth and bigness and power towards compassion and the re-knitting of human networks. Many others could be quoted to the same effect. A. H. Halsey met with widespread approval when he pointed out, in his Reith Lectures, that perhaps we have had rather too much liberty and equality, but not enough fraternity.[75] It should be added that not one of these authors is a theologian, or even a moral philosopher. Many are normally hard-headed economists who have been led by what they perceived to be the problem of modern society, to trespass into the field of (social) ethics.

Nor are the authors quoted so far conservatives. On the contrary, most would probably describe themselves as social democrats, even liberals. Needless to say, there is in the face of such a turn of events, a somewhat triumphant new conservatism as well. In some countries, it sails under the flag of a "reversal of trends,"[76] in others under that of a "new morality," or even a "moral majority."[77] Whereas the advocates of a social ethic are in fact seeking new ligatures, unheard of in the past, and designed to take the place of the values of modernity, that is of "rivalry" and "cupidity," the new conservatives seek to combine the classical industrial values of achievement and competition with the old ligatures of family, church, nation. Theirs is a truly reactionary position, a reaction against both the trend towards solidarity instead of achievement and that towards rationality instead of faith; they seek to revive a classical social Darwinism along with the Victorian virtues on which it may have been thriving a century ago. At least in popular appeal, the mixture is successful, though what it does to people's heads and hearts, is another matter.

The result of such trends and countertrends is confusing. As we try to unravel such confusion, the result is not pleasing. The search for ligatures is evidently one of the forces of our time. It tells a story about what is missing, but it does not tell us what is coming. For both routes which this search seems to take are equally suspicious. The "tender republic" which some of the German Greens advocate, has too many traces of that cultural pessimism which, when it turns to despair, can inspire the worst kind of politics.[78] Seeking Rousseau, finding Hobbes all over again. This is clearly not intended by many of those who advocate a new social ethic, but it is the pragmatic implication of an ethic of fraternity which tends to take the place of everything else, and in the process, abandons the blessings of modernity along with its contradictions. The "moral majority," on the other hand, is simply not credible. Its Darwinism runs counter even to the economic exigencies of the day, let alone to the social needs, and its Victorianism did not work even when it was real. Then, it concealed a reality of hidden licentiousness and corruption, it was hypocritical; today, it conceals the brutal grasp for power on the part of people who can barely pass the scrutiny of the American Senate, let alone that of God or His churches; it is pure politics.

Such bitter irony is not to be misunderstood. The problem with which we are dealing, is real enough, in theory as in practice. In theory, we have proposed a rather formal image of society. Norms, sanctions and power make for a cold world of metal railings, trap doors and bright neon lights. There is no need to retract for fear of the cold. This is, and will be, and should be a dimension of the real world in which we are living. Indeed, "in any society, some people will observe the law only under the threat of coercion and punishment."[79] But no society can work on the basis of such formal compliance alone. More than that, if people begin to "work to rule," the very rules by which they work will break down. Charles Silberman is therefore right in adding—in the context of criminal justice—that "in contemporary society, no less than in the past, the ultimate source of order is not coercion but custom and habit." This is not to say that custom and habit, the mores, can take the place of laws. "The point is that they are complementary: the stronger the mores, the more effective the laws tend to be." We need not only the protection of the laws against the unsociability of man, but we also need to build on man's sociability to make the laws work. This is where ligatures enter the picture. A society without ligatures is one faced with the alternative of Anomia or cold power. And of course, this is not an alternative, for the two feed on each other.

For in practice too, the apparently conflicting trends of the present are closer to each other than they appear to be in the hullabaloo of political debate. The very least that has to be said is that the "tender republic" and the "moral majority" feed on each other. When a social ethic begins to take the place of economics, the demand for the survival of the fittest is bound to arise somewhere, and with it, more likely than not, someone who defines what is meant by "fit," if not someone who selects those who are allowed to survive. This is not intended to insult those who have embarked on the long search for social bonds in a world without them. It may well be that some of the old bonds can be given a new lease of life; this is why Küng's synthesis of tradition and modernity is important. It may well be also that some of us have the strength, and opportunity, to weld new kinds of bonds which are not pseudo-ligatures; this is why Habermas's sophisticated advocacy of communities of free discourse is important. Also, it would be quite wrong to underestimate either the return of the sacred or the development of new forms of solidarity. But for the liberal, it is as well to remain sceptical.

We have argued that without fraternity there can be no society. But true fraternity is hard to come by in the modern world. It is well to keep one's senses rather that fall for one of the romantic illusions on offer in our time. We have argued also that without society there can be no liberty, or rather, we have begun to argue this point to which I shall return in my last lecture. Unless we accept social institutions as protection and opportunity for the unsociable sociability of man, we are not going to be free. The social contract, sanctions and all, is therefore a condition of liberty. But before we can complete the course of our argument, we have to look at the third wing of the triptych of the French Revolution, equality.

3. The Struggle for the Social Contract

Some people enjoy gloom and doom, others have reasons for it; but the majority prefer to look on the brighter side of things, and they have their reasons too. The countries of Europe and North America have experienced a long period of peace, at least at home. They have undergone an economic revolution which has led to unprecedented levels of prosperity for unprecedented numbers of people. They have seen their social opportunities of welfare, and their life chances more generally, expand almost without limit. They have found political stability in the form of a "democratic class struggle" of peacefully alternating parties which present their mildly divergent platforms to a mildly interested electorate. Occasional hiccups did not disturb the process unduly. there were of course distant wars in Korea, in Vietnam. There were conjunctural downturns, and the shock of the shocks of the 1970s. There was 1968 and all that. There was the assassination of one, and the resignation of another American president; there were minority governments and grand coalitions; France's Fourth Republic gave way to the Fifth. But throughout, the countries of the free world remained able to cope with such exigencies without jeopardising either their prosperity or their liberty. What then, if any, is the problem?

The answer is not as easy as it may seem, nor should we forget the background of stability and progress as we proceed to give it. Law and order may be a problem—but is it really more serious than the Vietnam war, or 1968, or the oil shocks of the 1970s? And is there any reason to believe that the free societies of the world will not be able to cope with this problem as they did with the others? Perhaps there is not. We shall try to avoid dogmatic answers to this as to all other questions. Yet as we look at the social fabric of our societies, we cannot but perceive some surprising and noteworthy strains. Prosperity, as measured by the customary yardstick of gross national product, is still increasing, but more than ten per cent. of those who seek work cannot find it, and important other groups see their real incomes shrink. Societies still offer more life chances to most but they do not seem to have a place for many of the young, or for those who have come from afar and knock at their doors. There are cracks even in the familiar political system, new parties, extra-parliamentary activities, demands for constitutional change.

Perhaps it is useful to start the story with the political process, to which it will also return because it is both expression and regulative force of the changes which are taking place. In the light of history, there is something deceptively mild about the notion of a "democratic class struggle." When S. M. Lipset applied the term in the 1950s, he assumed that political parties express underlying social conflicts.[1] These are, as a rule, class conflicts even if some parties do not like the word, class. "On a world scale, the principal generalisation which can be made is that parties are primarily based on either the lower classes or the middle and upper classes." "This generalisation," Lipset added, "even holds true for the American parties."[2] Everywhere there is a carefully regulated conflict between organisations based on the divergent interests of the haves and the have-nots.

In fact, to be sure, the process which led to the emergence of a *democratic* class conflict was long and painful; for a century or so, it was by no means clear that this would be its outcome; moreover, it was complicated everywhere by specific historical, cultural and institutional factors.

When the political economists of the eighteenth and early nineteenth centuries discovered the modern notion of class and the fact that a serious cleavage of social position and political interest is endemic in industrialised societies, they foresaw considerable threats to "the system" arising from this conflict. Marx gave the prospect his own twist, merging Scottish political economy and Swabian philosophy of history as only he could. Class conflict for him was not merely the struggle of divergent interests. It was a struggle the direction and outcome of which were determined by deeper historical forces. The haves naturally defend the status quo which gave them their position, and which they in turn had fought hard to attain when they were still have-nots. But the have-nots of the age are more than merely the dispossessed. They are also the representatives of new social forces, indeed of the force of the future. Whereas the haves defend existing relations of production, the have-nots speak in the name of forces of production which continue to grow in strength, until in the end they explode the edifice of existing conditions which holds them in check. In social and political terms, this means that the condition of the proletariat is bound to deteriorate until at the point of extreme "neediness" the "necessity" of dramatic revolutionary change becomes inescapable.[3] Others may not have followed this quintessentially philosophical figure of thought, but throughout the nineteenth century there was a widespread belief that the class struggle was bound to get worse, that is, more intense and more violent. What is more, there was every indication that this was in fact the case.

But then, two things happened. First it emerged that however important the new cleavages of class were—especially in Britain, for long the model country of both social analysis and social development—other social trends continued to affect the political process. Ruling classes remained divided, and preindustrial values, including a paternalistic concept of welfare, interfered with the harsher images of man and his motives painted by Adam Smith and Karl Marx.[4] The predicted levelling of the working class did not take place; distinctions of skill reappeared in new forms.[5] Agriculture did not disappear; in many countries, farmers and peasants remained an important social group and a critical political constituency. In any case, non-class determinants of political behaviour like religion blurred the clear lines of the picture. And of course there were those specific cultural traditions which led to, for Marxians, embarrassing questions such as those raised by Werner Sombart's *Why Is There No Socialism in the United States?*, or Thorstein Veblen's *Imperial Germany and the Industrial Revolution.*[6]

Even more important than these complications of the simple model of the class struggle were however the developments of this struggle itself, the process of what Theodor Geiger was to call the "institutionalisation of class conflict."[7] One cannot praise too often or too highly T. H. Marshall's analysis of this process in his *Citizenship and Social Class.*[8] One of the necessary conditions of industrial capitalism the right to conclude free contracts of labour, turned out to be a force for change. Equality before the law preceded or accompanied the industrial revolution. In the following century, the scene of battle moved from the legal to the political realm. The struggle for extending citizenship rights to political participation, notably in the form of universal suffrage, began. But this was not enough. Equality before the law and universal suffrage had to be backed up by the welfare state to be real. In Marshall's own words: "Civil rights gave legal powers whose use was drastically curtailed by class prejudice and lack of economic opportunity. Political rights gave potential power whose exercise demanded experience, organisation, and a change of ideas as to the proper functions of government. . . . The diminution of inequality strengthened the demand for its abolition, at least with regard to the essentials of social welfare. These aspirations have in part been met by incorporating social rights in the status of citizenship and thus creating a universal right to real income which is not proportionate to the market value of the claimant."[9] At the margin at least, economics was replaced by the law. The "democratic citizenship" thus created makes class distinction all but irrelevant.

The road to this end was of course bumpier and less direct than such general analysis suggests. In Germany, notorious faultings of old and new found expression in the process. Bismarck actually invented the modern Welfare State while at the same time preventing universal suffrage, or indeed the organisation of trade unions and a socialist party. In the United States, the welfare state has never been wholly accepted as a necessary part of a developed notion of citizenship. These caveats are important if only because they demonstrate how social analysis tends to overlook the very differences which are most important for real people in real situations.

Yet social analysis has its own power, as I hope to demonstrate. Our interest in this lecture is less in class inequalities as such then in class conflict and its political expression. Here, the first thing to notice is that progress with respect to citizenship rights was nowhere simply the outcome of the political organisation of class conflicts. Keith Middlemas has shown, in his *Politics in Industrial Society*, how important the two great wars of this century have been for advancing both political and social rights.[10] In a sense, universal suffrage was the "reward" for the contribution of the underprivileged to the efforts of the First World War, and the Welfare State was the corresponding "reward" after the Second World War. But when all is said and done, the organised expression of an underlying conflict of class interest by political parties and their contest has been the main motive force of social progress in the industrial world.

This democratic class struggle was, to be sure, both cause and effect of the process of extending citizenship rights. Without freedom of association there could be no socialist parties, without universal suffrage, they could not win elections. One can sense here the historic role of progressive liberal parties including their strange death.[11] Indeed, if one takes a very long view, the advancement of the open society and its political counterpart, democracy, may well have been the most significant subject of socio-political change in the last two centuries. And how painful it was! The battle with authoritarian traditions was difficult enough; and the later it was won, the higher was the human price which had to paid for it. Yet in our own century we learned the hard way that this battle had been harmless by comparison to the fight against totalitarian temptations. If only for that reason, one should not use the expression, democratic class struggle, lightly, or dismiss the achievements which it represents.

In the 1950s and 1960s, these achievements came to be recognised in most advanced countries of the free world. There were in the main two parties, one defending the status quo, the other demanding a better deal for the underdogs. These parties competed for electoral support with essentially similar chances of victory. They conducted their competition within accepted constitutional rules. Thus, civil war, or the threat of it, had turned into a fairly civilised contest. It had even made theories of politics possible such as Joseph Schumpeter first espoused and Kenneth Arrow and his disciples developed further, according to which market models of economic analysis can be applied to the political process.[12] At some point after the Second World War, Britain and the United States, the temperate Commonwealth countries, most countries of Continental Europe this side of the Iron Curtain, and one or two others came close to this model.

Before we continue the story, it seems useful to get one concept a little clearer which we have used throughout these lectures in a rather relaxed manner, although it carries a heavy burden of intellectual history, the concept of social contract. Even now, I do not intend to give it too heavy a meaning. Clearly, there is no implication of worthy men solemnly signing a contract, nor even of one of those great acts of confederation as the Swiss promulgated when they met on the Rigi to become Swiss, or the Americans in Philadelphia when they became Americans. In that sense, the social contract is no more than a manner of speaking. I prefer it to the more common concept of social order, because of the "part played by the social contract in the struggle for freedom."[13] It certainly seems more in line with the unsociable sociability of man. Of course, Rousseau used it too, and indeed introduced the general will to explain it; but this merely goes to show that there is no pristine language left for us epigones. The social contract signifies the unspoken agreement to abide by certain elementary norms and accept the monopoly of violence on the part of a common power set up to protect these norms. (We have observed earlier that in this perspective, the distinction between a "contract of association" and a "contract of domination" is redundant.[14]) This unspoken agreement will never include everybody, though it is binding for all; on the other hand, it could not hold if it was not backed up by the bonds which arise from man's sociability. The wording of the contract is never final. Articles can be added to it, and perhaps also taken out. The process of extending citizenship right in response to the class struggles of the last two centuries can be seen as an amendment of the social contract. The minimal and the maximal state (which are what the wording of the social contract is about) will concern us again as we come to discuss society and liberty. But whatever the answer, the general notion of norms and sanctions and power which are subject to consent if not consensus, and glued together by the bonds of culture seems sufficiently useful to retain it.

If we apply this notion to the story of class in industrial society, one circumstance stands out. In modern class conflicts, the social contract was not the issue, indeed it was never really at issue. There is one exception. As long as these class struggles had a genuinely revolutionary potential—never in the United States, perhaps before 1889 or so in Britain, and until 1919 elsewhere[15]—there was always the possibility of that momentary suspension of the social contract which is the hallmark of revolutionary transformations. But such extremes apart, the edifice of capitalist or bourgeois society was the accepted context of the struggle. This may sound surprising at first. Of course, the forces of change wanted to gut this edifice and refurbish it from top to bottom according to their lights, and in fact they did so to the point at which neither "capitalist" nor "bourgeois" describes what modern societies are about. But none of this altered the common context in which the classes operated. Characteristically, even the most radical analysis, that by Marx, describes the classes as locked into each other in a common predicament. The bourgeoisie needed the proletariat to produce its wealth and sustain its power, and the proletariat needed the bourgeoisie to develop its potential. The class struggle is, in the strict Kantian sense, one of those "antagonisms *within society*" which are the source of all progress.[16]

Naturally, as the refurbishing process went on, and the haves and have-nots of yesteryear began to co-operate to make their common edifice habitable, their conflicts lost in intensity and violence. The democratic class struggle ensued. Indeed, when Lipset wrote his analysis of modern politics, the notion was already beginning to lose its meaning. Progressively, the political process no longer deserved the name, class struggle, at all. In this connection, one change had special significance. Citizenship meant choice. It meant participation and a decent income, and it also meant mobility. Geographical mobility was in one sense a precondition of the labour contract on which capitalism was based; though in the early stages, this was forced as much as voluntary migration. But now social mobility proper was added to the picture. Some of it had always existed; Peter Bauer is right to point out that totally closed social strata are doomed to paralysis and soon, extinction.[17] However, in advancing industrial societies, opportunities and risks of mobility expanded to an unheard-of measure. Moreover, they were mostly opportunities; individual moves on a given scale of income and status were accompanied by an upward drift of the scale itself. Largely at the expense of the old working class, the "new middle class" emerged, that amorphous but rapidly growing social category which, while not the seat of power, was nevertheless clearly distinct from the proletariat of old.[18] In the United States, mobility, and a middle class image of society, were almost founding principles of the commonwealth; after all, with the exception of the American blacks, all citizens had moved from somewhere attracted by the American dream of unlimited possibilities, and for many decades, the frontier within remained open.

This is Sombart's subject.[19] His thesis is that socialism was absent in the United States because people did not need to join forces with others in order to improve their lot; they could do so by their own efforts and achievements. With the Americanisation of modern life, the experience spread, albeit mitigated by very different cultural and institutional traditions. More and more, people all over the industrial world preferred to rely on their own ability to get on rather than the promises of reforms, let alone revolution, by political parties and movements. Class struggles and the resulting political con-

flicts were to some considerable extent converted
into individual competition. Social mobility became
the new expression of the antagonisms of society.[20]
As a result, class and party allegiances declined. The
floating voter became the political equivalent of the
democratic citizen. Political conflict turned into a
game of the kind described by Anthony Downs in his
Economic Theory of Democracy: political parties
trying to maximise support by offering packages of
promises which appeal to the preferences of rational
voters.[21]

But is this true? Even Downs is at pains to point
out that he is proposing a more or less useful model
rather than describe reality. Electoral research
shows that to the present day, major parties can rely
on a reservoir of supporters who are loyal come what
may, and prefer to suffer for their party rather than
switch allegiance. Moreover, opportunities for
mobility are far from universal. Self-recruitment at
the top and lack of opportunity at the bottom of the
scales of stratification are familiar phenomena. If we
therefore take another hard look at our story, its
point turns out to be a somewhat different one.

The image of politics and society which was so
widespread when every other social analyst seemed
to write about the "end of ideology" was probably
no more wrong than that of open societies with
democratic citizens able to advance their life chances
by individual effort which I have presented here. [22]
But it was right only as a summary of a historical process. This began with the gradual organisation of the
class struggle between the haves and the have-nots of
power and privilege in industrial society, led through

a phase of "institutionalisation" or "democratisation" of this struggle to the social changes which involved an ever more effective encroachment of citizenship on social class. At the end of the line, however, there is not the eternal repetition of the party game as a positive-sum game for all, but the emergence of a very large category of democratic citizens, people who would probably describe themselves as middle-class, and who benefit from a system for which even the mild term, democratic class struggle, is too fierce. These two-thirds, possibly three-quarters of all citizens of modern free societies have a common interest in the maintenance of political institutions which guarantee economic growth and social peace; their divergent interests are comparatively minor; moreover, such differences do not lend themselves to the formation of classes and class-based parties. Indeed, in a relevant sense, this majority, silent or otherwise, but by preference silent, is one class with all the internal distinctions and differences which have always been characteristic of classes. If one likes paradox, one might call it the citizens' class; the more common name is, middle class; this is of course also the "one nation" class, the class of "consensus politics" and all that, including the other "social contract." At times one might be forgiven for simply calling it, *the* class; it is in any case the majority class.

For there are no others besides it, no classes that is, though there are significant groups and categories which flavour the political process. In the first place, there are the remnants of an older condition, authoritarian or traditional upper-class elements who have usually withdrawn to their estates which nowadays include Marbella and Acapulco, and traditional proletarian groups whose members wonder whether they will ever be assured of their citizenship rights which seem to come and go with the tides of conjuncture. In other words, even in its own terms, the majority class still has much to do. But it is the beginning of a new story rather than the completion of an old one which has led us into this tale in the first place. This new story not only takes us straight back to the issues of law and order, but it also guides us to the social and political problem of our time.

This problem is the unintended, but also inevitable result of the old story of citizenship rights. Once again, modernity has generated contradictions which provide the agenda for the future. Take the Welfare State, that final stone in the arch which holds up the roof of the edifice of citizenship. The Welfare State—or as I prefer to call it in order to avoid misleading connotations of paternalism: the social state—is a system of resource transfer designed to guarantee the effectiveness of citizenship rights for all. Its emphasis, its methods, even its extension differ from country to country[23]; but everywhere the system itself has given rise to problems which cannot be resolved within the principles on which it is based.

Two of these problems stand out; they concern the resources available for transfer, and the ways in which this transfer is brought about. A variety of contingent and inevitable developments have conspired to make the resources available inadequate for the objective foreseen. The assumption that the social state will remedy past injustices and therefore become progressively cheaper has turned out to be sadly wrong. In fact, technical developments in medicine, but also in education, and of course rising real incomes for those administering the social state, were alone sufficient to bring about a cost explosion. If one adds the fact which is stated here without any implied criticism that often *l'appetit vient en mangeant*, that demand is created by the availability of services, the explosion becomes even greater. Unforeseen demographic developments have not helped. Coupled with profound changes in the world of work (to which we will turn presently) they have meant that fewer and fewer people have to finance the citizenship rights of more and more. In the meantime, taxation has reached levels at which, "Laffer curve" or not, further increases of tax rates are not likely to yield more revenue, if only because of their effect on the economy. The point is worth noting. In a sense, social policy obstructs the very dynamics of modern economies which it presupposes in order to be affordable. In any case, the 1970s have made the vulnerability of growth-based economies apparent. The result of all these trends is a dilemma of entitlements and resources which plainly cannot be contained.

This is not made easier by a parallel dilemma of structure. While every social problem is ultimately a problem for individuals, any public response to it is bound to be general. Social policy without bureaucracy is unthinkable. But setting up the bureaucracies of the social state has all kinds of unintended consequences. For one thing it means that a costly element of friction is built into the transfer of resources. More and more people get back as much as they paid in taxes, minus the cost of those who administer the transfer. For another thing, the nature of the beast, bureaucracy, is such that it misses the very individuality of the cases which it is intended to remedy. Bureaucracies, and the rules and regulations on which they are based, have to reconstruct the individual case from general principles, and this cannot succeed as well as good neighbourliness and compassion do. In the end, human beings feel that they are but numbers in a game which is not theirs. Weber's nightmare of the "cage of bondage" in which modern man ends up as an inevitable result of the process of "rationalisation" becomes real.[24]

What is to be done? There are many answers to this question, and they are not all discouraging. But one point is certain. It is that the increase in resources available for transfer has to be arrested, and that at the very least there will have to be a stabilisation of the proportion of gross national product spent on social expenditure while demands and entitlements are rapidly rising. As we know today, this is happening everywhere. The political complexion of governments may make a difference to the extent of such cuts and above all the climate which they create; some advocates of supply-side economics and the new social Darwinism seem positively delighted with the need to curb the social state, whereas social democrats try to play the cuts down as mere adjustments of the system; but everywhere the process goes on. Thus the next question is: whom does it hit? It is hard to avoid the answer: not the members of the majority class.

Even in the mid-1970s, when stagflation rather than

unemployment was the major topic of concern, there were those who pointed to the "new social problem." "The old social problem between employers and workers is in principle and in institutional terms under control. Not so the New Social Problem between those who are organised (*e.g.* producers) and those who are not (*e.g.* consumers)."[25] Perhaps, consumers were not the most convincing illustration. In the mid-1980s in which the notion of a "new poverty" has for good, or rather for bad reasons gained wide currency,[26] we know much more precisely where the problem lies. Frank Field lists seven major "groups in poverty"[27]: the unemployed, the old, single-parent families, sick and disabled people, the low paid, single women with aged dependants, and poor people in institutions. Except for the low paid, they are all largely dependent on transfer incomes. They are therefore all hit by curbs in public expenditure, or even in its growth. They are by the same token victims of simultaneous developments with which most of those in employment can cope in one way or another, such as increases in value-added tax, in the cost of transportation, and above all in the cost of housing. The new poor are characteristically those who are least able to defend themselves as the social state reduces its benefits.

To be sure, the majority class does not remain entirely unscathed. From higher prescription charges to the conversion of student grants into loans, from the reduction of certain family benefits to those of housing subsidies, measures have been proposed or taken which affect those earning regular incomes as well as those dependent on transfers. But for one thing, it was always strange that the benefits of the social state should increase for those with regularly growing real incomes, and for another, the new burdens rarely exceed the increasing ability of those in stable employment to pay. Even students continue to have expectations of lifetime earnings which are a multiple of those of the majority of taxpayers who used to finance their grants. The majority class looks after itself, to the extent of cutting benefits for people at or beyond the margin, but defending the jobs of those who administer the benefits; schools and hospitals close, but school and hospital administrators stay. The clear effect of this process has been well put by Meinhard Miegal when he speaks of a "new polarisation," but "not so much between the richest and the poorest as between the poorest and those strata of the population who are slightly better off than the average."[28] The crucial boundary is that between the majority class and those who are being defined out of the edifice of citizenship.

How many of them are there? This is a nice debating point for those who are concerned with definitions of poverty. I do not propose to get involved here in the question of how "relative" poverty has to be to be called, poverty.[29] By the standards of Calcutta, many of the poor of Britain and Germany and the United States may still be reasonably provided; their physical survival is not at risk; but equally it is probable that about 10 per cent. of the population of the richest countries of the world have barely enough to sustain themselves, and considerably less than a decent life would require.

Nor is this the whole story by any means. Many of the new poor are pensioners, members of incomplete households, or people who have in some way been unlucky in life and have not found a way back into the majority class. But a growing number are unemployed, the bulk of whom is not included in the ten per cent. figure but would have to be added to it. Mass unemployment is a relatively recent phenomenon. In 1975, the proportion of those seeking employment in the ten member states of the European Community who were without a job, was 4.5 per cent. By 1980, unemployment in Europe had risen to 7.5 per cent., and by 1985, to 11 per cent. It is thus understandable that many economists and politicians regard the phenomenon as temporary and seek to link it to essentially conjunctural processes. Against that, it seems to me that we are in fact faced with a development which deserves the name, "new unemployment." Its causes and ramifications run much deeper than passing cycles of economic success or failure, and the remedies are therefore much harder to come by.

In part, this thesis is born out by statistics. The proportion of long-term unemployed who have been registered as such for over a year, and are often no longer in receipt of unemployment benefits, has risen rapidly, typically (in Europe) from 10 per cent. to thirty per cent. of those registered as unemployed in the last 10 years. Moreover, regional differences are not only striking, but show up regions with a persistent proportion of 20 per cent. and more unemployed. Everywhere, there is a hidden figure of people out of work which is high. But statistics apart, one fact is beyond dispute even among the most anti-structural economists: over the last 60 years or so, that is since the introduction of the eight-hour working day, there has been a systematic reduction in the per capita hours of paid employment needed to sustain the growing economies of advanced countries. The phrase is carefully chosen. There has not necessarily been a decline in the total number of hours worked; the labour market itself has expanded in most countries, and continues to do so in some. But the individual lifetime contribution to the total employment effort of economies has gone down significantly, possibly by so much as one-half in the last 60 years.

For a long time, and especially in the last 40 years, this process involved the realisation of ancient dreams. More time was set aside for the initial period of education, the retirement age was lowered, paid holidays were extended, the working week was shortened, to say nothing of a more generous attitude to absenteeism as well as to breaks during working days. All this benefited those at work; it meant a new balance of work and other activities of life. In some cases, it even meant the infusion of the spirit of free activity into the world of work. The whole process was accompanied by, if not based on nearly continuous increases in real incomes both by growing real wages and by higher transfer incomes for most. But from a certain point onwards, this gigantic positive-sum game ceased to work. First there was stagflation eating into the incomes of many, though more of those not in paid employment than others. Then, boom unemployment reared its head. The reduction in paid employment led to a division into those who continued to have jobs and those who were defined out. At first, it appeared that they would be defined out for a limited period only; but as economies began to pick up again after an extended slump, it became apparent that now growth was possible without clearing the labour market. Figures were bandied about: when does growth lead to significant reductions in unemployment? At three per cent? Four per cent? The fact is, we do not know; but we do know that the growth rates which we can expect, and which are fairly high especially if they are re-translated into actual volumes of goods and services, will not lead to significant reductions of unemployment. As a matter of fact, the majority class does not need the unemployed to maintain and even increase its standard of living.

This is a tough and even an objectionable statement, but unless we appreciate it, we will not come to grips with modern social problem. In the *Communist Manifesto*, there is the important, if at first sight somewhat cryptic statement: "To the extent to which the bourgeoisie, that is capital, develops, to that extent does the proletariat develop, that class of modern workers who live only as long as they find work, and who find work only as long as their labour adds to the value of capital."[30] It is this kind of statement which I had in mind when I argued earlier that the Marxian classes were locked into each other. They needed each other for their survival as such. Marx or no Marx, even at the time of the great depression—to say nothing of that of the Korean War when unemployment was also very high—there was no question but that economic recovery would be indissolubly linked to getting people back to work. It would require re-employment, and it would result in re-employment, as indeed it did every-where. Today, this is no longer the case. The major-ity class can live perfectly well, including new cars every three or four years, holidays in Spain, annual real increases in wages and salaries, and relaxed debates about where the cuts in social expenditure should fall, without unemployment ever falling much below 10 per cent.[31] There are those who are in and those who are out, and those who are out are not needed.

It is easy to hear the clamour of objections even as this lecture is written in the quiet of a comfortable study. How can anyone say that human beings are not needed? Is the unemployment problem not simply one of social rigidities which could soon be solved by a new flexibility of wages and conditions of employment? Is it not an illusion to believe that the majority can live perfectly well with 10 per cent. unemployed? Will they not rise and destroy the edi-fice of the many? There are answers, even to the one question which is often not asked, namely, whether work is so desirable that it should be turned into the overriding objective of concern and of action. If we are so rich, and can get richer with less employment, should we not be thinking about creation and distri-bution of wealth rather than that of work? Can we not break out of the curious capitalist-socialist con-spiracy which cannot imagine a world without the discipline of employment? Or is this one of the unshakeable creeds of the dominant majority class as well?

Perhaps the most appropriate way of answering at least some of these questions in the present context is by returning to the story of class. What we are saying is that the process of citizenship and the emergence of a majority class has in fact led to the creation of a "two-thirds' society" (to use a term current in the German debate on the subject[32]). Two-thirds, and perhaps even more, are "in;" they enjoy the full benefits of citizenship including the growing welfare offered by a prosperous economy. But in the process, they have defined out a sizeable number from these benefits, more that 10 per cent. certainly, and perhaps as many as one-third. Of course, these could be used, as cheap labour for example; but there is no place for them in the scheme of citizenship. They are what Americans call, a new "underclass."

The "underclass" can be described in many different ways, not just by listing the "new poor" and the "new unemployed." Lord Scarman has included in his report on *The Brixton Disorders*, a chapter concerned with the "disorder and social policy" which contains stunning descriptions of deprivation as well as some recommendations of remedies.[33] The inner city is one of his subjects, the ethnic minorities the other. Both are notorious problems in the United States, and in a more limited way in Continental Europe as well. Bad housing, insufficient nutrition, virtually non-existent medical care, the absence of effective education, no employment, coupled with social stigmatisation and discrimination combine to produce that desolate mixture of misery, illiteracy, lack of purpose and of cohesion, and of course crime, which is characteristic of the Bronx in New York, of parts of London, Liverpool, Glasgow, and in a more hidden, shamefaced way of Continental cities as well.

This too does not describe the "underclass" many of whose members would not admit to their position either to others or even to themselves. Probably, the only inclusive way to describe it is negatively. The "underclass" consists of those whom the full citizens of society do not need. They are either not citizens, or no longer citizens, or no longer full citizens, or not yet citizens. The first applies to immigrants, especially if their citizenship is still an issue. The second applies to the old, though in their case there are complicating factors. One is that in the social state their place is safeguarded by a "contract between generations," that is by those able and working making sure of their own future by protecting the present of the retired. The other is that demographic processes and changes in the world of work have made the old an increasingly important constituency. They do not have to organise themselves as "grey panthers" to be seen and heard. Yet the loosening of bonds and the resulting invisibility of many pensioners, means that old people are vulnerable. Those who are no longer fully citizens are the dropouts, of whom there have for some time been more than a few picturesque *clochards* under the bridges of the Seine. If one adds those who were sick, or had accidents, or came into conflict with the law, or just could not stand the pace, a category of considerable size emerges.

But by far the most important part of this category is that of those who are not yet citizens. They are of course, the young. Charles Silberman speaks of "children [who] find themselves adrift in a cultural no man's land."[34] Many young people do indeed. There has always, at least in all societies in which places of work are separate from homes and schools, been a gap between the process of socialisation and training, and the initiation into "real life." At times, the gap was very small indeed, as for the children employed in coal mines and factories in nineteenth century England, though it was always relatively big for the better-to-do. With increasing prosperity, their pattern has become the model. Today, the gap has assumed frightening proportions. At its far end, as it were, the work society is receding, less prepared or capable to accommodate young people at the age of 16 or 18. Can one be surprised that they see themselves as a "no future" generation? At its beginning, on the other hand, a growing uncertainty has taken hold of the institution of socialisation. More often than not, families—in so far as there are complete families at all—shrug their shoulders of 14-year-olds; schools have frequently ceased to be able to offer anything of interest, and formal discipline has all but broken down. The no-man's-land which thus emerges may span four, six, even eight years for the social construction of which modern society has almost nothing to offer. In the absence of norms, and of ligatures, it is really surprising how many get through the no-man's-land unhurt. Youth culture itself may well be a clue to the answer.

In the meantime, a significant proportion of the young remain outside the edifice of citizenship in the "underclass." This fact more than any raises the question of whether we are talking about a class at all. The answer is that we are not. Although the social process of marginalisation is systematic, the resulting category is precisely not a class, that is it does not have the potential of organisation derived from the strength of a wave of the future on the crest of which it is riding. In fact, it is not riding on such a wave. Not even the young represent the future. It is true that one of the striking features of the new "underclass," and notably of its youthful element is that instead of orienting itself to the values of the official society and trying to climb aboard, it seems not only resigned to its fate but actually attracts some of those near the margin to its style of life, drugs and crime included. The underclass is infectious.[35] There are those who almost hide the fact that they have jobs, and hurry back to roam the streets with their unemployed pals. Even so, no productive force informs this category. In sociological terms, and without wishing to add insult to injury, the "underclass" is not a class, but a *lumpenproletariat*.

Marx used this term to describe what he called "that passive rotting-away of the lowest strata of the old society" which will "be sucked into the movement here and there by a proletarian revolution, but which by its whole condition of life will be more prepared to allow itself to be bought for reactionary activities."[36] The remark is perceptive. Theodor Geiger developed it in his early explanation of the successes of National Socialism in Germany. He spoke of the "rabid rebelliousness" produced by extreme deprivation. "Communism and National Socialism have a much easier time in these quarters than the *realpolitik* of social democracy and unions."[37] And again: "There is, as we know, a sediment of the working population who do not find a place in employment, have lost the ability for a steady life, and therefore hire themselves out without asking in whose interest they use their fists, clubs and knuckles."[38]

The main point about this category—for want of a better word we shall continue to call it, "underclass"—is that its destiny is perceived as hopeless. It is not seen as resulting from an attempt on the part of ruling groups to hold down a potential for change, but as a kind of final judgment of definition. This in turn leads to reactions which are fundamentally individual and situational. That is to say, members of the "underclass" are a reserve army for demonstrations and manifestations, including soccer violence, race riots, and running battles with the police, but they are not a revolutionary force. They stand for nothing, even though they may stand against everything. As quickly as they assemble, they will also disperse; their assemblies do not last, just as their actions have no future and no past. They may be effective while they take place, but they are meaningless if compared to the class struggle of the last century.

But then, the comparison is misleading. Clearly, this is the point at which the cultural analysis of the last lecture, and the social analysis of the present one, can be linked to throw some light on the problem of law and order described at the outset. If societies tend towards the weakening of norms by spreading impunity, and to the loosening of the bonds which express the sociability of man's unsociable nature, and if they define a sizeable proportion of their potential members out of the entitlements and benefits of membership into an unprotected social space, then the climate is rife for crime. Riot and rebellion, and those other mass phenomena which escape social sanctions, are one facet of the condition; but the other is, straightforward individual delinquency, crimes against property and against persons. To some, this may be a relatively easy trade, the mirror image of the work society, as the ("not very successful") crook explains with respect to the miners (who were then on strike): "I'm a bit of an underground worker myself, only they wouldn't catch me down a coalmine in a million years."[39] The more relevant point is that "they" would not catch him anyway. To others, crime is a more desperate way out of misery, and it usually does not work. But to the official society, it is that great threat to one of the cherished values of the citizens' world, law and order.

For this is the crucial point about the process of marginalisation that it turns the social contract into the dominant issue. Contrary to the class struggle, the incongruous antagonism between a fairly well organised majority class and an amorphous "underclass" which pops up here and there and elsewhere, at Luton Town football ground and in a Grunwick picket line, but also in one's home when one has been away on holiday and in a subway train late at night, raises questions about the fundamentals of social order while it defies all traditional methods of containment and institutionalisation.

Here we reach the point at which it is no longer true to say that the majority does not need that other third. The harsh divisions of economic life give rise to a desperate struggle in social and political terms. For while it may be true that the *lumpenproletariat* is a "*passive* rotting away" of those at the margin, it is also an unmistakable reminder of the precarious legitimacy of social order. This group varies in size; at times it shrinks to a tiny percentage of misfits and victims of ill fortune, at other times it grows into a large "underclass." When the latter happens, the alarm signals of legitimacy are out.[40] Crises of legitimacy always have something to do with the inability of societies to engender loyalty for their basic values. If these values become self-destructive, the crisis is there for anyone to see. We have repeatedly used the term, citizenship, in a strictly impermissible way, to describe the privileges of the "two-thirds" by contrast to the deprivation of the "underclass." If citizenship turns out to divide rather than to unite, it has lost its force. More than that, the very assumptions of the official society, of its norms and sanctions and structures of authority are in jeopardy. This is what the struggle for the social contract means. It is not only a running battle with the police, but a struggle with everything that the majority stands for. Only, the struggle has all the disturbing qualities of guerilla warfare. The issue is clear enough; it is the social contract; but all traditional methods of coping with conflict—trade unions and wage bargaining, political parties, elections and parliamentary debates—must fail.

How then does the majority class react to this predicament? The continuation of our story is as fascinating as it is worrying. In the first instance, the
majority class reacts by closing ranks. Many of the
rigidities which have been described as characteris-
tics of modern societies can be understood in this
context. Mancur Olson gave us a very American
analysis along these lines, a continuation almost of
the economic theory of democracy. He says that
"special interest groups" have an inherent tendency
to form cartels (he calls them "distributional coalitions") which make innovation and growth difficult.
"Distributional coalitions generate slow decision-
making, crowded agendas, and cluttered bargaining
tables. . . . Special-interest groups bring about
sticky wages and prices."[41] The longer stable democratic conditions prevail, the more impenetrable does
the glue of special-interest groups become. There is
an "inherent conflict between the colossal economic
and political advantages of peace and stability and
the longer-term losses that come from the accumu-
lating networks of distributional coalitions that can
survive only in stable environments."[42] Not only
economies grow, but nations "rise" when they are
flexible and open, whereas they "decline" when they
become rigid. Max Weber's vision of the bureau-
cratic "cage of bondage" was equally gloomy, if
more European in style. Weber too saw above all the
price which we would have to pay for the progressive
rigidity of social conditions. How is it possible (he
asked) to retain any "individualistic freedom of
manoeuvre" in the face of bureaucracy? How can we
be sure that there are powers which hold bureau-

cracies in check? Where do the politicians and entre-
preneurs of tomorrow come from?[43]

Clearly, it is a matter of great moment where the
sources of innovation are in a rigid world. But innovation does not by itself cope with the other cost of
rigidity, the struggle for the social contract. Here,
the closing of ranks on the part of the majority class
has been highly effective. Miegel is clearly right in
his summary:

> "As relevant studies show, the prevailing mood
> has for some time been this: Improvements of
> the economic position of needy strata of the
> population—yes, but not at our expense. Trade
> unions have to fight against this prevailing mood
> if the improvement of the employment situation
> which they hope to achieve by shorter working
> weeks leads to reductions in real incomes with
> the employed. The majority follows such a stra-
> tegy unwillingly, if at all.
>
> This attitude is at present characteristic for
> the political majorities of nearly all industrial
> countries. Wherever a more uniform distribu-
> tion of income and wealth has been sought in
> recent years, as in France, this attempt met with
> a surprisingly strong resistance in the popula-
> tion. Conversely, governments which not only
> tolerate considerable differences in income and
> wealth, but openly advocate them, as in Britain
> or the United States, enjoy remarkable appro-
> val.
>
> Contrary to the 'seventies, it appears that the
> 'eighties are not a time for handing out, but
> gathering in."[44]

Can anyone be surprised that the so-called fight against unemployment produces so many words, and so few actions?

But the closing of ranks on the part of the citizens is not all. Most of them dislike the fact that a new "underclass" has emerged. They find poverty distasteful, unemployment a violation of their own underlying values of work and achievement, and crime abhorrent. As a result, a certain restlessness sets in which turns people against those whose stake in the status quo is too obvious. The victims of this restlessness are bureaucrats, but also trade unionists and generally the "familiar faces" which have now become "old faces" because one seems to have seen them around forever. People want something new to happen, anything almost. Innovation becomes a goal in itself.

Thus we are back to the questions raised by Max Weber and much later by Olson and others: who is, by virtue of social position and opportunity, not prepared to pay the price of ossification for the comforts of the status quo, but seeks to break the prevailing rigidities in order to find new horizons? Identifying new social forces has become a favourite game of social analysts at least since E. Lederer and J. Marschak discovered the "new middle class" in the 1920s.[45] Since then, the "service class" (K. Renner), the "managerial revolution" (J. Burnham), those whose "capital" is education (P. Bourdieu) and many others have had to serve the purpose.[46] They have not done well; all these groups have happily merged with the majority class. However, a more convincing case was made by Daniel Bell in his *Coming of Post-*

Industrial Society.[47] Bell was well aware of the rigidities of a bureaucratised world, and he looked round for new social forces in the strict sense of Marx's forces of production. He concluded that "the major source of structural change in society—the change in the modes of innovation in relation of science to technology and in public policy—is the change in the character of knowledge: the exponential growth and branching of science, the rise of a new intellectual technology, the creation of systematic research through R & D budgets, and, as the calyx of all this, the condition of theoretical knowledge."[48] If "the roots of post-industrial society lie in the inexorable influence of science on productive methods," it follows that "the scientific estate—its ethos and its organisation—is the monad that contains within itself the imago of the future society."[49]

So far, so good. Many would agree more than a decade after Bell's book that the main source of innovation is science and technology—the "information revolution"—and that those who handle this process one way or another must therefore be the heralds of the future. They may not be confined to the "scientific estate," indeed they may have little concern with "the codification of theoretical knowledge," but they have a wave on the crest of which they can ride, and its name is, technology. But what does their new-found confidence have to do with the "underclass"? In some respects, the "post-industrial society" is a great distraction. Since vague, but great hopes attach to it, the impression is created by some that if only we embark on this new route, all problems, unemployment included, will be solved. Yet it is easy to see that the new technological age will of itself contribute to defining out considerable parts of the population who are either no longer needed because computers have taken over their work, or can no longer be used because they lack the training and perhaps the capacity to cope with the alienated world of electronics. It may be that we have to, and want to go ahead into the information age, but in doing so we carry with us the burden of the age of citizenship which will not disappear overnight.

At this point, the as yet nameless groups who represent and sustain the new confidence of advanced technology, split down the middle. There are those who combine a technocratic view of progress with a sense of compassion. After a year or two of traditional left-wing policies in office, the French socialists have moved in this direction which of course was that of the American Presidential hopeful Gary Hart and his *yuppie* supporters. But not all "innovators" are yuppies. Greater strength, and most certainly greater noise emanates from that other group which one might call, the social Darwinists. They combine the belief in the innovative force of high technology with the attempt to revive the alleged or real creeds of Victorians. Once again, there are the pessimists who believe that "men have to face up to the inherent hardship of the battle of life" and those others who "promise that, whatever the immediate hardships for a large portion of mankind, evolution meant progress and thus assured that the whole process of life was tending toward some very remote but altogether glorious consummation."[50] Richard Hofstadter, from whose study of social Darwinism this is quoted, adds a little later: "We may wonder whether, in the entire history of thought, there was ever a conservatism so utterly progressive as this."[51]

Without doubt, the progressive conservatives, whoever they are in terms of social position and economic potential, are the stronger group. They are also the main source of the active pursuit of those policies which are commonly associated with the terms, law and order. Poverty and deprivation (they believe) are by and large people's own fault. There are enough examples of whole groups working their way out of misery by their own efforts; just look at Asian immigrants by comparison to West Indians. Crime is an unacceptable stain on the clean slate of an orderly society, quite apart from restricting the lives of law-abiding citizens in an unbearable way. What one needs, is not "wet" theories which try to explain crime away by reference to social conditions but tough and effective action, the "short, sharp treatment" of young offenders, harsher sentences for persistent delinquents, severe penalties for hooligans and those who allow them to do their dirty work, and strict police control wherever there seems to be a no-go area, whether social or territorial.

Such views are not as easily dismissed as some would like it, although we shall argue that while the road to Anomia is paved with impunity, it is not enough to try and re-establish sanctions pure and simple in a world in which anomy has so many concomitant causes. But in terms of the struggle for the social contract, the politics of law and order fits well into the picture which we have here presented. In all advanced societies, there is an overwhelming majority of people who do rather well by what economy, state and society have to offer. They differ in the degree of their satisfaction; haggling for a share of the cake is still continuing; but by and large they could also live with the indexing not only of their incomes but also of their rights to participation, their opportunities for mobility, their life chances more generally. The *scala mobile*, the escalator is the perfect symbol to describe the society of the majority.[52] Its political expression is the implicit coalition of all major parties, the strain towards consensus which has been noted even in the most excetric political system, that of Britain. Consensus politics is, or rather was, the dominant feature of advanced societies after the successful conclusion of the democratic class struggle.

It was never complete, to be sure—less so in some countries than an others—but above all it did not last. At one end of the spectrum, traditional socialist parties increasingly came to be torn between acceptance of the fact that their supporters too had become citizens, members of the majority class, and the inclination to adopt the cause of those at the margin, or even the "underclass" itself. Since it could not represent itself, it had to be represented: a very Marxian, in effect authoritarian figure of thought.[53] The new concern is helped by the fact that the "underclass" is such a cocktail of interests. Concern for the deprivation of "groups in poverty," the rights of minorities, the "maltreatment" of alleged offenders by the police, can be mixed with elements of youth culture, "alternative" values, ecology rather than economy, and the mixture can quite plausibly be represented by those who spend their comfortable majority class lives with those at the margin or beyond, local government officers, social workers, teachers.

At the other end of the spectrum, conservative parties by and large still represent the upmarket end of the majority class. Their supporters at any rate prefer to operate "inside right" rather than on the right wing.[54] They combine the desire to keep the economy going with the belief that co-operation between social groups is the foundation of stability and thus a strong defence of an affordable social state. Compassion for the disadvantaged motivates them as much as the hope that a generous attitude to those who violate rules will in the end bear fruit. But these conservative "wets" while dominant in numbers, are no longer necessarily dominant in influence. A harsher group of Darwinists has begun to take over conservative parties. The triangle of high technology, supply-side economics and law and order politics with an element of "new patriotism" thrown in, gives them considerable strength. They may be the group which turns the threat to the social contract into an actual struggle.

For this should by now be evident: the peaceful picture of modern societies with which we have begun our story is both apt and deceptive. It is apt in that the majority of citizens can probably continue to enjoy the life chances brought by modernity for some considerable time to come. There is no revolution in sight, nor even a new class conflict which might disrupt peace and quiet. But the picture is also deceptive. All of a sudden, citizenship has become an exclusive rather than in inclusive concept. But of course those who are denied full citizenship rights by the very strengths of these rights and their contradictions—by what must be called Welfare State poverty, or work society unemployment, that is poverty and unemployment actually resulting from the social state and the work society—do not go away. They remain a reminder of the precariousness of the social contract, and more, they are a festering sore which increasingly infects the social order as a whole. For a while, advocates of the technological revolution may distract attention from this inflammatory process. For a while, mild antibiotics dispensed by the majority class may keep it at bay. But in the end, societies will either get to the root of the problem or run the risk of abandoning liberty in the search of unambiguous answers. For this is the stark alternative: a radical liberalism, or the threat of a new wave of totalitarian temptations.

I hope no one expects me to outline the programme of a radical liberalism at the end of a complex, and at least in intention, largely non-partisan analysis. Clearly, certain libertarian principles remain valid. Their application to minorities, ethnic or otherwise, remains a major objective. Equally clearly a radical liberalism would have to be oriented towards the future. It cannot, and should not resist the technological changes which are among the few forces which promise to help us pry open the modern cage of bondage. It cannot, and should not resist the new desire for decentralisation either, although the balance between decentralisation and centralisation, between local and international needs may well be a specifically liberal task. Moreover, in these as in other respects, not resisting is not enough; one would like to see liberals in the vanguard of innovation.

Beyond that, answers will have to be given to two of the social issues to which we have alluded in our analysis. One is, the position of the young. A society which defines out the old, lacks compassion; but a society which omits to define in the young, or worse, which systematically keeps them out, lacks a sense of its own future. What is needed here, are of course not palliatives, welcome as they may be. A limited scheme for youth opportunities plus some incentives for vocational training and a few discos supervised by priests are fine, but not enough. A whole new attitude is needed. This may include provision for a "national social service," but only if it is clearly understood that its purpose is neither to discipline the young nor to undercut the wages of those in employment, but to introduce a new kind of tax, as it were, a tax on time to make sure that the many things which need to be done but which no one does in the normal course of things, are done.

In any case, the other urgent answer concerns the future of work. Economists and politicians are allergic to Hannah Arendt's phrase that the work society is running out of work.[55] They point out that there will always be enough to do, and of course to that extent they are right. But they are not right to suggest that all that needs to be done is to lower the cost of work; citizenship is not for sale. Nor are they right to confuse paid employment with human activity. The two can be combined and ideally this should be the case in more and more fields of employment. In any case, the extension of free activity remains a worthy purpose. But as long as we have not been able to think through the economics of a society of activity, the task remains to distribute the work—the employment—that is available in such a way that the present dividing line between those who have work and those who do not is abolished as quickly as possible.

These tasks are hard enough. In fact, we have only named them and not proposed any remedies. But there remains the hardest task of all, a radical liberal response to the problem of law and order. One can understand the complaints of those on the left who deplore what they call, "the theft of an issue" in view of the monopolisation of the debate on law and order by the right.[56] It is less easy to follow the argument that more of the same approach coupled with a social and economic policy to combat poverty and unemployment will do the the trick. It will not. The causes of the problem of law and order are, as I have tried to show in the last two lectures, many. They range from the application of Rousseau to criminal law through the externalities of citizenship to the social as much as the economic condition of the "underclass." A liberal response can therefore neither just advocate more of the same old Rousseauean medicine nor the replacement of the law by social and economic policy. It will have to involve an attitude to institutions which is both firm and restrained.

4. Society and Liberty

———————————

The answer to the problem of law and order can be put in one word, institution-building. This may not seem very striking nor very practical; it is certainly not a patent medicine; but it is a liberal response, and perhaps the only one which deserves the name. Only by a conscious effort to build and rebuild institutions, can we hope to secure our freedom in the face of Anomia. The rest of this final lecture on law and order will be concerned with what this means and does not mean, how it is achieved, and what might happen if we fail in the process.

Institutions—what are they? "Order," says Werner Maihofer, "is a structure of relations of things or persons."[1] This seems plain enough. There are persons, and there are things, and the social contract regulates the relations between persons as well as those between persons and things. John Locke had it all: "And thus the Commonwealth comes by a power to set down what punishment shall belong to the several transgressions which they think worthy of

it committed amongst the members of that society—
which is the power of making laws—as well as it has
the power to punish any injury done unto any of its
members by any one that is not of it . . . ."[2] Citizenship, sanctions, norms, authority: the territory is
familiar.

But is it really just a territory of "relations"
between persons and things? It may be so, but then,
"man can maintain a permanent relationship to himself and to others only indirectly, he must find himself by a detour stepping out of himself, and that is
where institutions are located."[3] This is Arnold
Gehlen, and it is about the "location," perhaps the
nature of institutions: "If we lift off the rules of
mutual behaviour, we get the blueprint of a lasting
arrangement, an institution."[4] In other words, institutions are not just relations, they have their own
separate existence, detached, or at any rate detach-
able from relations with things or persons. One
should perhaps not probe the word "existence" too
hard in this context; it reminds one of Durkheim's
"social facts" which led him into all kinds of trouble.
Suffice it to say that institutions can be very hard
"objects" indeed if we bump into them by not playing our part in the social drama of life.

Is "institution" then just another word for norms
and sanctions, "valid" norms and sanctions perhaps?
One might be tempted to think so. After all, Justinian's *Institutiones* were the textbook of his *corpus
iuris*, a collection of laws and penalties for the benefit of students and probably judges as well. But then
institution-building would be any addition to this
textbook, any traffic regulation introduced by a local

authority, including the wheel clamps invested to enforce compliance. This makes little sense, although it makes some sense, because clearly institutions have something to do with norms and sanctions.

John Locke, in tracing his way to the social contract, does two things. One is that he defines certain relations as privileged—one to persons, the physical integrity of the individual, and one to things, the protection of property. The other is that he goes to great lengths trying to explain why norms and sanctions relating to physical violence and to theft are important. Even in the state of nature, he argues, "every man has a power to kill a murderer," "a power" implying not only the ability but also the right.[5] So far as property is concerned, it is the fruit of human labour which in turn is God's command, and "he that in obedience to this command of God subdued, tilled, and sowed any part of [the earth], thereby annexed to it something that was his property, which another had no title to, nor could without injury take from him . . . ."[6] This sounds quaint to us, but the gist of the argument remains useful to the understanding of institutions: they define "a power" or "a title"; the notion should be confined to certain privileged norms, among them definitely those providing for the protection of the person and certain aspects of property; and these are norms for which reasons can be given which refer to fundamentals of social order.

Lest this be misunderstood as a treatise rather than an analysis, let me introduce a note of controversial interpretation. In the early stages of post-

1968 terrorism in West Germany, there was much debate about the boundary between "violence against things" and "violence against persons," and at first, the former was regarded as acceptable, the latter not. But the whole debate rested on the error that "order is a structure of relations of things or persons." In one crucial respect there is no difference between setting a department store on fire on a Sunday when there is nobody in it, and killing a businessman and his bodyguards with sub-machine guns. Both acts involve "violence against institutions." They violate not just codified institutional claims to the "protection of the state" or to "public order," but the normative construction of society itself. Since they are chosen for their visibility, one must assume that precisely this was the intention; but this in turn must mean that the response is about protecting institutions rather than persons or things.

But what is one protecting if not the norms relating to the fundamentals of social order? Any answer to this question runs the risk of sounding metaphysical. Even Montesquieu had to resort to the "*spirit* of the laws" which is an important part of what we are talking about.[7] Norms can be mere paragraphs in a textbook of law, but they can also be living, meaningful rules which are somehow at one with the principles from which they follow, whether they are in fact derived from them or not. If "the mind of the laws" was not such an awkward phrase, it would be preferable as a translation of *esprit*. Certainly norms can be mindless; in other words, not all laws and rules deserve the name, institutions. But perhaps Arnold Gehlen has caught best what we have in mind by exchanging metaphysics for architecture and speaking about the "blueprint" of norms. The word suggests both real laws and an underlying deep structure, that is the normative construction of society from its principles; this combination of fact and meaning describes institutions.

It also helps us understand the notion of institution-building. Institution-building is the creation, and often the re-creation, of meaningful norms from their principles. At times it involves merely a new process of reasoning, of giving reasons why it should be right to act in accordance with certain rules. At other times it leads to significant changes in actual norms and sanctions. Sometimes it is a process of reviving memories, of re-linking the present with the past; as often it is a design into the future, a task of reform. In many cases, the linking of laws and their spirit is not just an abstract task of the mind, but one that requires almost tangible arrangements, law courts and local police stations, vocational schools and social benefits for one-parent families. Colloquially, such arrangements are often taken for the institutions which are housed in them; the concreteness can be misleading but is not necessarily mistaken. Anyway, we shall give examples of these and other practical ways of institution-building presently.

Before that, one short, though (for the author) painful detour helps clarifying the issue. Why should institutions thus defined be worth protecting, let alone building? The answer is, because of the unsociable sociability of man. Institutions protect us from the untamed lust of others for things and for power. They enable us to put our sympathy for others to good purpose. Above all, however, they provide the framework within which the "antagonism" which motivates much human action can be turned into a force for progress. It is only within institutions that we can hope to improve our life chances. Institutions are not just a necessary condition of liberty, as constitutions are a necessary condition of effective human rights and the systematic control of power, but they are also the material which needs to be moulded and shaped to give expression to the desire for more freedom for more people. We cannot be free without institutions, and freedom means that we build institutions according to our lights.

At this point, a personal note is in place. In these lectures, I have attacked several friends. Now I have to add myself to this list. The institutional liberalism which I am advocating here is incompatible with the views which I took in an enthusiastic but youthful piece which unfortunately still finds its readers, *Homo Sociologicus*. In this long essay, I summarised some of the knowledge of the time (the essay was written in 1958) concerning social roles. "All the world's a stage, and all the men and women merely players . . . ." I also took a somewhat involved methodological position. On the one hand I argued that constructions of the scientific mind, like *homo oeconomicus*, or indeed *homo sociologicus*, were never intended to describe the nature of man. On the other hand I added, the scholar cannot evade the practical consequences of his models; he is responsible even for the misunderstandings of others. In order to avoid such misunderstandings, I wanted to distinguish clearly between man the player of roles, and real man. From the latter's point of view, society was a vexatious fact, and freedom could only be gained against it. "Only if the sociologist selects his research projects with an eye to what may help liberate the individual from the vexations of society, if he formulates his hypotheses with a view to extending men's range of free choice, if he does not shy away from supporting political changes designed to increase individual freedom, and if he never forgets the superior rights of Herr Schmidt the person over his role-playing shadow—only then can he hope to use the insights of sociology to protect man the inhabitant of the earth from the boundless demands of man the inhabitant of a country."[8]

The essay found many critics, all of whom I refuted conclusively in another paper entitled, "Sociology and Human Nature," except that today I believe that my critics were too lenient with me. They omitted to castigate me for my contribution to turning sociology into the study of sub-institutional, if non anti-institutional aspects of human behaviour (or even the anti-institutional study of behaviour). More generously still, they did not link my views to the manner in which a whole generation of students, many of them students of sociology, fell out with institutions and came to attack them. What the critics had to say, was bad enough. One colleague mocked my piece by reminding me that "moralizing has at all times been the greatest enemy of theory."[9] Another colleague, the philosopher-sociologist Hulmuth Plessner, found the thesis of *Homo Sociologicus* "spoken right out of the soul of German

'inwardness' " and added: "If in order to make the
sphere of freedom unassailable we identify it with
that of privacy (and privacy, we should note, in an
extra-social sense), freedom loses all contact with
reality, all possibility of social realisation."[10]
Plessner was right with respect to the effects, if not to
the motives of my essay.

At first sight, the assumed antagonism of *homo
sociologicus* and "autonomous man" might appear
to be the very opposite of Werner Maihofer's image
of man's "being himself by being as" a bearer of
social roles.[11] Indeed there is a difference. The
anarchist streak of "sociological man" has little in
common with the barren conformity of "the meaning
of social order." Yet the first sight is misleading. We
have seen that in fact Maihofer is guided by the
notion of the essential goodness of man, and "socialised man" the conformist is a mere excuse for his
sins. Conversely, my absolute contrast leaves society
as a world of conformity almost without exit, a kind
of 1984. The mistake is the same in both cases, a failure to understand not only the need for institutions,
but their libertarian opportunities. If we want to be
free, we have to work with and through institutions,
shaping and re-shaping them in the process, that is
building them in the image of the chances of liberty
open to us at any one time.

This still leaves the question: what institutions? It
is time that we return to the starting point of this
analysis, law and order. We have referred to
increases in crime, both perceived and real, in the
last 30 years. We have shown that there is something
systematic about this process in that recent decades

have also seen a progressive relaxation of sanctions. This is how breaches of norms are related to power and its legitimacy. We have then gone on to discuss the context which explains this process of de-legitimation, or the increasing precariousness of the social contract. One line of explanation led us to the prevailing image of man (in fact to the other, the anti-social side of *homo sociologicus*) and its application in criminal justice and elsewhere. Another line took us to the marginalisation and eventually the defining-out of an "underclass" which embodies the doubt in the validity of the social contract. The answer, we said, cannot lie with economic and social policy alone, important though both are to respond to the problems of the social state, of the young, and the unemployed in a world which is no longer dominated by work.

None of this—to repeat an important point—explains why particular persons at particular times commit crimes. We may have described the social and cultural climate in which crime is likely to thrive, and law and order are at risk, but this description provides neither causalities nor excuses for acts which need to be looked at on their merits. By the same token, the debate about sentencing, penalties and prisons is not directly relevant to our argument. We are moving neither in the field of criminology nor in that of penology. The relevance of the punishment of offenders in our context is solely as an example of institution-building, its motives, its purposes and effects.

Thus we grant that retribution and revenge, "an eye for an eye," are rather unworthy motives of punishment, though I should not dismiss out of hand John Locke's principle: "Each transgression may be punished to that degree and with so much severity as will suffice to make it an ill bargain to the offender, give him cause to repent, and terrify others from doing the like."[12] So far as terrifying others is concerned, we have of course much evidence which shows that this has little relation to common preconceptions. D. Archer and R. Gartner have recently "proved" once again that, in the case of homicide and the abolition of the death penalty at least, comparative evidence is conclusive: "In this cross-national sample, abolition was followed more often than not by absolute *decreases* in homicide rates, not by the increases predicted by deterrence theory."[13] Once again, there is no need for us to re-open this dossier.

The case of "correction" or "re-socialisation," and also the case *for* such an approach is a little more difficult, because in one rarely discussed respect it is directly related to our concern. What exactly does re-socialisation mean if the society to which offenders are supposed to be returned does not exist? There are two sides to this coin, too, though curiously they are identical. One is that prisons and other detention centres are mirror images of the surrounding society, with perhaps a notable "under-class" element, and not places of discipline and order as those who have never been in them might think.[14] The other side is that even if offenders in detention were told of the values of an orderly social life, they would find little in the real world to confirm such textbook lyrics. After all, what is one to "socialise" a young person for, if it is clear that he will go back to a broken home in a slum district without a chance of a job and with all his friends and pals in much the same position? However, even this observation is no argument against trying; it is merely a caveat arising from our analysis of the "underclass" in a world of anomy.

"The American correctional system today," an official commission found, "appears to offer minimum protection to the public and maximum harm to the offender."[15] This may well be so in other countries also. But if we grant all this—where does institution-building begin? In the first instance, with an argument, an intellectual case. Criminology and penology are in the nature of their scientific programmes about the individual. This is as it should be. It is clearly also right that judges should be guided, in their sentencing practice, not only by the letter of the law or the literal force of precedent, but by their assessment of the individual offender and his circumstances. Discretion is and should be used to make sure that justice is done in a particular case. *Fiat iustitia, vivat persona.* It is never a good idea to sacrifice the world for a principle.

But discretion can, and should be more than a balance of specific rules and specific, individual circumstances. There is a third factor, as it were, which deserves greater prominence than it has been given in recent decades. It is the preservation of institutions. By this I explicitly do not mean those rules and norms which are concerned with public order and the protection of the state, nor is it implied that the preservation of institutions will as such deter anyone from committing particular offences. I mean the notion that the norms and sanctions by which men have chosen to regulate their affairs are themselves a cultural achievement worth protecting, and the need to build confidence in institutions among those who may never be tempted to commit a serious crime. The individualisation of penal practice has by the same token de-legalised it somewhat, or put differently, by paying more attention to specific, often personal circumstances judges and others involved in dispensing sanctions have turned away from the merely formal application of norms. I am advocating a certain de-individualisation of the penal process, not by a return to legalism, but by increased awareness of the need for, and the needs of institutions.

Does this mean harsher sentences? It might, though much of the scepticism with regard to the effect of punishment which pervades the literature on the subject is probably justified. The death penalty does not deter murderers, and prisons do not deter thieves. Thirty years of detention do not "improve" a person any more than five, and the cases in which detention of a particular person actually protects many others from injury, are rare. But unless (if the pun be permitted) judges show the courage of their convictions, a climate of nonchalance with respect to institutions will spread in society which benefits neither those who are part of the edifice of citizenship nor those whom they have kept in the cold. If anything goes, nothing makes sense any more, and if nothing makes sense, one may as well break the law or ignore it. A sense of institutional responsibility has to be joined to respect for the law and regard for the individual offender and his victims in order to reconstruct the social contract.

It is no misunderstanding of this position to infer that I regard the extreme leniency which goes with a purely individualistic understanding of punishment as wrong. A penal theory which abhors detention to the point of replacing it totally by fines and useful work, by "restrictions of the standard of living," is not only intellectually flawed because it confuses law and economics, but also socially wrong.[16] It sacrifices society to the individual. This may sound unobjectionable, even desirable to some. But it also means that such an approach sacrifices certain chances of liberty to uncertain personal gain. Being nice to offenders may bring out the hidden sociability in some of them, but it will discourage many who are far from the criminal scene from contributing to the perennial process of freedom which consists in sustaining and shaping the institutions which men have created.

A policy of law and order after all? Whoever has listened carefully, will know that this is not what our argument is about. For one thing, we do not fall victim to the fallacy of misplaced concreteness in this respect. Enlarging the police force, dispensing short, sharp treatment to the young, re-introducing the death penalty will not solve any problem, least of all the overriding issue of law and order. The least we can learn from modern penology is a considered approach to the practicalities of crime prevention, punishment and correction. For another thing, we do not advocate the return from an individualising, compassionate and psychological approach to offenders, to the resurrection of formal principles and letters of the law. Such a reaction is undoubtedly as tempting to many as the reversal of trends is more generally, but it is also as misguided and costly. As in the case of the Welfare State and in others, it will merely re-create the problems of yesterday which we have successfully overcome. It also misses the task of institution-building which is about meaning as much as formal norm. Our plea is for a third element in the sanctioning process, a sense of institutional continuity.

Recently, a friend of mine—will there be any friends left after these lectures?—who is a well-known scholar and writer, was arrested for obstruction in connection with a peace demonstration outside an American air base. Before the local court he argued that since he was morally right and the government was wrong to allow the deployment of Pershing missiles, it was an abuse of the law to fine him or sentence him to detention. (His argument was of course somewhat more elegantly put.) In the event he was fined, but the local judge used the occasion to make a simple point. My friend, he argued, had every right to express his views about the nuclear threat and also about the morality of a government which did not seem to care. But invoking a higher legitimacy against the law, can "pave the way for totalitarian trends which we both reject." The demand for impunity was something quite different from a civil disobedience which involves limited violations of rules and accepts legal sanctions for it. To what end will the battle for the waiver of sanctions lead? To be sure, the nuclear challenge is unique in its seriousness; to meet it, political, legal, moral and religious efforts are needed. "But human life is essentially life in freedom which has to be reasserted all the time. It can certainly not be the meaning of history that it is extinguished in nuclear death, but that it falls prey to political totalitarianism cannot be its meaning either, especially since the latter would by no means be a guarantee for avoiding the former."[17] The local judge has said by example what I mean when I speak of introducing the third factor, the protection of institutions, into the relationship between the law and the individual; he has in fact contributed to institution-building in a wobbly world.

Few subjects are more obvious candidates for what Karl Mannheim called, the "suspicion of ideology" than punishment and social structure.[18] Thorsten Sellin may well be right in his pessimism when he argues that there is not really much difference between "retribution" and the "protection of society" when it comes to penal practice; all modes of punishment merely serve to defend the values of those in power.[19] Rusche and Kirchheimer trace this *motif* throughout penal history and conclude: "The penal system of any given society is not an isolated phenomenon subject only to its own special laws. It is an integral part of the whole social system, and shares its aspirations and its defects."[20] However, this is not an argument against the validity of certain positions at certain times. Even if it could be shown that our advocacy of institution-building serves the interests of those who have a stake in social order (whoever they are at a time at which the majority becomes the unintended cause of disorder) this would not be an argument against the project. More important still, it is perfectly possible that one approach, such as the individualisation of justice, was right at one time, whereas another is right today. Liberty is never achieved in one fell swoop, nor do we ever have it once and for all. We always have to move forward, and sometimes sideways too, to extend human life chances. Thus we would claim that the order of the day, no more, is institution-building without abandoning the gains of either the rule of law or respect for individual circumstances and needs.

Institution-building is of course not just an approach to the penal system. The next step takes us back to the "no-go areas" which we have described as characteristic of the road to Anomia.[21] There was first the propensity not to prosecute for certain crimes, like theft, and even to avoid detection for reasons which range from overloading the police and the courts to anticipating the waiver of sanctions on compassionate grounds. This will not do. Contractions of the criminal law are certainly possible, and in many cases, desirable. One of the great gains of recent changes has been the extent to which the private sphere of individuals has been removed from the eyes and ears of the law. (And, by the way, one of the great losses of recent technical developments has been the extent to which the eyes and ears of government agencies have intruded in this private sphere; there is new scope for the law here which must be filled in the interest of individual freedom.)

But where such contraction has not taken place, and should not take place because the fundamentals of the social contract are at stake, the law loses its institutional plausibility if it is not enforced. Going into this "no-go area" is a requirement of legitimacy. I do not know what the practicalities are in this respect, but dealing with them would certainly seem worthy of the efforts of the best.

Our second "no-go area" was that of youth. It is arguably the most important of all, and also the most difficult. We have already referred to the needs of education, vocational training, employment and meaningful activity. In terms of institution-building, two needs of young people stand out. One is that a society which takes citizenship rights seriously must make every effort to define its future members in, even at a cost, indeed preferably at a cost. This is probably a two-way process; it involves real opportunities of participation for the young, but also a reaching-out of the official society to their values and their culture. The other need is for the institutions which one wants to defend to be plausible. It is not enough to assert that they exist and must therefore prevail; reasons have to be given which persuade those who are doubtful, whether they are young or black or just poor. If such reasons are hard to find, change may be necessary. Many norms and values may need shaking up to regain plausibility. Here, a great leap is needed from a combination of wobbly withdrawal from responsibility and empty assertion of status to authority in the full sense of the word.

It is more than an aside to mention in this connection the institutions of democracy. They are badly in need of re-constitution in view of two contrasting yet related trends, and unless they are re-constituted their legitimacy will fade with their plausibility. On the one hand, there has been a trend towards "democratisation," by which is generally meant the greater participation of all in everything. This trend was clearly a logical extension of the advancement of citizenship, but like so many other extensions of a desirable process, it has produced contradictions which tend to defeat its original objective. Once general participation is taken beyond a certain point, it results in immobility, indeed in the unmovability of the political system. General participation creates veto groups, and whatever the majority mildly wants, can be stopped by the veto of activists. General participation may even create a veto mood among non-activists as well. Some of the rigidity of contemporary societies is the direct result of their "democratisation." On the other hand, and not surprisingly, this discovery has given rise to a new wave of anti-democratic thinking. It is latent in most countries, though open in France, and implicit in many demands for firmer government and clearer leadership.[22]

Institution-building in this respect has to begin with first principles. Democracy is about seeking progress in a world of uncertainty. Its constitution must make change possible, but remove it from arbitrary acts of the few. This means that it must create conditions for initiative but also for control, and both must be related to the rights and interests of citizens. For a long time, control was the problem; authoritarianism was government by arrogated if benevolent power. But today, the main problem is one of initiative. Institutions must encourage initiative without denying the mechanisms of control. Max Weber saw this problem long before others; it is still with us.[23] What is more, it is with us not only with respect to parliament and government, but in all other institutions too, although the constitutional arrangements needed in business enterprises, armies, or universities are bound to differ from those of the political society.

But let us return to the "no-go areas" of the law. There are, thirdly, the no-go areas proper, districts and organisations and also occasions, which appear to be out of bounds for the forces of the law. They take us for a last time to the important subject of community development. Here as in so many respects, the liberal has to walk a tightrope, and is always at risk to fall off on one side or the other. We have taken issue with a "communitarian" approach which holds against lawlessness and disorder the idea "that an extension of democratic activity and participation must be sought and encouraged, since chaos or repression are the unattractive, but probable alternatives."[24] Participation through "community forums" in the "primary cells" of society with a view to "education" and the creation of a "communitarian ethic," so it is hoped, get to the roots of crime. The probability is that it will not. It will deliver the task of law and order to sub-institutional activities. By relying too much on the sociability of man, it will remain exposed to the unsociable acts of the few, and perhaps not so few. The result will be either centralised repression—a fear which certainly seems justified—or the use of private power, that is the war of all against all, including vigilante groups against criminal gangs.

Whoever wants liberty, has to have the courage to seek a third way. This too may well begin at the community level. As much decentralisation as possible should certainly be sought. Much can be done here, including "activities designed to deal with direct causes of crime" (*e.g.* by providing employment for ex-offenders) "activities by citizens to improve the criminal justice system" (*e.g.* by police advisory councils), "activities that rely on reducing opportunities for crime" (*e.g.* what in the United States is called "target hardening"), and "programmes aimed at assisting the victims of crime."[25] Moreover, it is highly desirable to strengthen the role of local communities more generally, because ultimately they are the only effective source of social as against political or even police control. But none of this makes sense without effective forms of policing, including of course a close connection of the police with local communities, and above all, without an institutional approach to law and order. This is why the evidence given to Lord Scarman's inquiry by the Lambeth Council for Community Relations is so important: "If there be any persons—and there may be—who believe that crimes should go unpunished because they are committed by persons of a particular shade of skin, the Council are not of their number. If there are any who believe that some of the violence to person and property which accompanied the Brixton disturbances were the legitimate self-expression of an oppressed minority, the Council do not share these beliefs."[26] Institution-

building with respect to no-go areas means supporting the institutions of the law by filling the inters-
tices with a sense of community. It does not mean
taking the law into one's own hand, not even into
the hands of democratic communitarian groups, but
using one's own hand to uphold the spirit of the
law.

Finally, there was the difficult "no-go area" of
riots. It is difficult because riots elude in the nature
of the case our capacity to cope. In fact, all forms
of uncontrolled mass action are a reminder of the
vulnerability of institutions. We should therefore
have no illusions; there is no way to prevent them
nor is there a method for stopping them quickly
short of unacceptable terror from above. More than
other challenges to law and order, riots require a
calm and assured institutional sense. Lord Scarman,
in his report on the Brixton disorders and as a prac-
tising judge, provides a supreme example of this
attitude. In the Brixton report, he goes through a
number of practical needs of "police handling of
disorder," including "effective re-inforcement,"
"increased training," "protective equipment,"
"vehicles for transporting officers," and "improved
arrangements for communications," Scarman
obviously realises how inadequate such improvements are bound to be in an extreme situation, but
he adds that this should not lead to hysterical
changes. He remains sceptical of "water cannons, CS
gas, and plastic bullets," and instead insists that "it is
vital that the traditional appearance and role of the
British police officer is preserved, as far as possible,
in the public order role of the police as in other

aspects of their duties." "It would be tragic if attempts, central to the thrust of my Report, to bring the police and the public closer together, were to be accompanied by changes in the manner of policing disorder which served only to distance the police further from the public."[27] It is hard to think of a better example of the spirit of institution-building.

There is much that institution-building cannot do. For instance, it cannot achieve quick results. As an attitude as much as a programme of action, it needs time, and so do the changes which ensue. Institutions are not built in a day. The process is no substitute for economic and social policy either. We do not recommend institution-building instead of vocational training for the young, or a re-thinking of the Welfare State. Both are needed, and it is as wrong to use institution-building as an excuse for inactivity in matters of economic and social policy, as it is to believe that such policies make the building of institutions redundant.[28] Institution-building is also not a substitute for the rule of law. The point is important. The rule of law in the sense of a set of formal rights for all and the due process to defend them is one of the great achievements of human history. It is a liberal achievement, not in any party sense, but in the sense of the progress of liberty.

The rule of law can probably not work, and can certainly not work well, without a sense of institutions in a society, indeed without it becoming itself institutional in the full meaning of the word. Throughout these lectures, we have insisted on the shortcomings of the formal law as such. But this is not to detract from its strengths. There is much to be said for the common law tradition which combines formalisation with live institutional meaning, but there is enough to be said for codified law to make it a desirable objective for people everywhere. The law protects, and the law enables; institutions give significance, substance and permanence to its powers. Quite apart from institution-building, the law needs to be developed in order to make its rule fruitful for freedom; data protection is but one contemporary example.

If institution-building is no substitute for what can be done by deliberate, in the widest sense political action, it is no alternative for what has to grow and eludes deliberate acti n, that is for ligatures either. At the end of the second lecture, we have left a question mark over the future of these deeper cultural bonds without which the social contract is ultimately not worth the paper on which it is written (if that is not extending a manner of speaking too far). The whole point about them is that they cannot be manufactured. Social policy can be manufactured in this sense, and even institutions can be built as the German local judge and the English Lord of Appeal who we have quoted, demonstrate. They can be built by all of us, judges or mere citizens. But ligatures need their time. Perhaps, a climate of intact institutions is more favourable to their emergence than one of anomy. One would certainly hope that institutions create a receptivity for real rather than pseudo-ligatures, and that this is a side-effect of institution-building. But the gap remains. Modern societies will have to be held together by more precarious bonds than ligatures for the foreseeable future, and they will therefore remain precarious themselves.

Institution-building is thus a modest step forward. Still, it is the only one at our disposal so far as the heartland of law and order is concerned. This still leaves us with a question which we have held in abeyance for some time. It was first put in defining the relation between law and social policy: how can the proper sphere of the law be defined for a free society? What is the role of sanctions not only in relation to law, but to liberty?[29] To these we have added in the present context: to what extent is institution-building desirable? Within which limits are institutions both a condition and a vehicle of liberty? Throughout, we have viewed the social contract from the vantage point of Anomia; it is time that we should look at it from the other end, that is, from hypernomia, of the greediness of norms which threaten to suffocate all initiative and freedom.

Robert Nozick does not like the term, social contract. He prefers the invisible hand which was invented once the civil wars of the seventeenth century had faded into history and progress seemed possible by relying on the market. But this is a mere quirk of terminology if one remembers that the social contract is no more than a manner of speaking. Even Nozick who regards the case for anarchy as strong—"why not have anarchy?"[30] he asks, and he finds that "formulating sufficient conditions for the existence of the state thus turns out to be a difficult and messy task"[31]—in the end comes to define a small sphere of absolute norms on this side of which the beneficent malevolence of market forces is not allowed to rule freely. Once he has found the way, not without difficulty, from anarchy to "protective associations," from their battle to a "dominant protective association" and on to the "ultra-minimal state" which protects on the principle of insurance rather than by entitlement, he does admit the "minimal state" which he has defined at the outset: "Our main conclusions about the state are that a minimal state, limited to the narrow functions of protection against force, theft, fraud, enforcement of contracts, and so on, is justified; that any more extensive state will violate persons' rights not to be forced to do certain things, and is unjustified; and that the minimal state is inspiring as well as rights."[32]

Nozick is least convincing where he is "inspired" and waxes lyrical about his creation ("treating us with respect by respecting our rights, [the minimal state] allows us, individually or with whom we choose, to choose our life and to realize our ends and our conception of ourselves . . . "[33]) but the hard core of his argument contains three lessons in our context. The first is a reminder. Institution-building demands that we give reasons, take nothing for granted just because it exists and has been around for some time, but at the same time do not abandon the search for good reasons because of a vague preference for the assumed sweetness of an unprotected life without institutions. Institutions matter.

The second lesson from Nozick is an emphatic restatement of a point which we have made in other ways. The need for institution-building does not mean that the more institutions there are, the better the world is. Institutions have to be necessary to serve their purposes. Such necessity cannot be demonstrated except in a limited number of cases. Anomia is not the only danger, the other is what we have called, hypernomia, the wild growth of norms and sanctions and institutions. So far as norms are concerned, the phenomenon is familiar. While many legislators get themselves elected for the first time by arguing that there are too many laws already and that greater simplicity and transparency of norms is urgent, they soon join with their longer-serving colleagues in proudly counting the number of laws they have enacted as an index of achievement. As a result, our law books, the modern equivalent of Justinian's *Institutiones*, are cluttered with texts which confuse rather than clarify, spread uncertainty rather than certainty, and weaken confidence in the institutions of the law by not being applied. Perhaps it has always been true that employees could bring economic life to a standstill by "working to rule"; however, the trick has probably never worked as quickly or as perfectly as at this time at which the plethora of sometimes incompatible rules and often unenforceable sanctions makes immobility likely even without any special effort to comply with the letter of the law.

The conclusion is that there are times when institution-building may mean adding to the list, others when it means re-construction, but also those when concentration is more important than extension. This is probably a time for re-construction and concentration. We need not more institutions but stronger ones and probably fewer than stake a claim for support in contemporary societies. Even if the time for de-institutionalisation is past, institution-building should proceed sparingly and with due regard not only to reasons but to necessities too.

This leads to the third lesson of Nozick's argument and one where he may well be wrong. Not all institutions have to be derived from one first principle—indeed such Cartesian consistency would be suspicious—but it is useful to form a view about the minimum of normative and institutional answers which the social contract has to provide. Nozick's view is (almost) clear. It is "the protection against force, theft, fraud enforcement of contract, and so on." Thus he confines his justification of norms and institutions to Locke's basic "powers" and "titles" (arguing as he does from a Lockean state of nature[34]) but includes the first groundrule for enabling his minimal citizens to conclude contracts with each other. That he also adds an indefinite "and so on" is a surprising lapse of weakness in a disciplined and precise thinker.

Or is it merely honest? At any rate, Nozick would not wish to go beyond what I should describe as Article One of the social contract which has to do with the protection of life and limb. In particular, he would not accept an Article Two which stipulates that the contracting parties will make a joint effort to see to it that the basic rights of membership—citizenship rights—are guaranteed for all. This takes us into the domain of Nozick's *bêtes noires*, Herbert Hart and John Rawls, and to the argument that the social contract is about "justice as fairness' rather than about libertarian rights.[35] Nozick turns the argument into a case of Reagan versus Mondale, or perhaps Thatcher versus Kinnock. He suggests that the advo-

cates of justice believe that the less well-off make
their social co-operation dependent on a transfer of
resources when in fact "constraints upon voluntary
social cooperation" in the name of fairness mean
"that those already benefiting most from this general
cooperation benefit even more."[36] In other words,
justice does not work. So let the "working poor"
fend for themselves, and the non-working poor "get
on their bikes and find work" (one is tempted to
extrapolate). "No one has a right to something
whose realisation requires certain uses of things and
activities which other people have rights and entitlements over."[37]

Countering Nozick's arguments is by no means
easy. It is particularly difficult if one shares his pre-
occupation with liberty (he would say: individual
rights) as the first objective of the social contract, or
even of the minimal state. But there are two extreme
cases which give pause. One is the possibility for a
few to exploit their unusual accumulation of "rights
and entitlements," such as property, and restrict the
effective ability of others to make use of their rights.
This is not a question of economics; it is one where
the economic advantage of some turns into a legal
disadvantage of others. Even recent history is replete
with examples of such conversions of wealth into
power which it is hard to justify. The other extreme
is that of members of a society who are denied the
effective entitlement to participate by lack of fundamental opportunities of education, of information,
and above all of sustenance. This is the more difficult
case. It raises a question which should not be dismissed too lightly: why are the poor poor? But it is at

least possible that in some cases or in some respects, affirmative action is needed to enable members of society to become citizens. Article Two of the social contract would take care of this need.

Robert Nozick has an endearing way of apologizing for his arguments against good sense. He too is concerned about parting company with his friends.[38] For us, this is hardly a worry which we can hold against him. Yet there is a point where his sophistication turns into sophistry. True, the "minimal state" is a more catching notion than, say, the "optimal state"; but then these are matters where to be catching may not be enough. As we proceed to rebuild and to concentrate institutions, we can do worse than to be guided by an idea of the state which entails the monopoly of power *and* the guarantee of citizenship. "How dare any state do more?" to use Nozick's language. "Or less."[39] In other words, we are still talking about a reduced state, and about sparingly building institutions, but so far as the essential rights of citizenship are concerned, justice is not absent from the normative construction of society.

To some this may seem strange language about important matters on which there are controversial views. What about human rights for example? They are, in the normal usage of the term, a part of the optimal state. The European Convention of Human Rights (or some equivalent) should be part of national law everywhere. This too is a task of institution-building. And what about the social state? Here we move into an area where the contraction of institutions may well be part of a new credibility, that is of legitimacy. But it is equally clear that we are seeking a new social state rather than a non-social state. And law and order? It should be obvious by now that whereas the class struggle of the past century was primarily about economics, the struggle for the social contract is about law. However desirable the redistribution of wealth or of work may be as a condition of citizenship, it will not solve the new social problem. The struggle for the social contract is won or lost by our ability to build institutions which stem the tide of anomy.

Erecting buildings is fine, and even the frustrations of construction work can be compensated by satisfaction if one sees one's blueprint, one's plan slowly come to fruition—but what about those who live in these buildings? Clearly institutions, like norms, are but a shell, abstract creatures which come to life when people act within and towards them. We all act within and towards institutions, but in certain roles we have special responsibilities for them. This is why one further step of the argument would be to examine "the personality of lawyers" and "the politics of the judiciary" (to cite two titles of important books on the subject[40]). It is by no means lawyers only who are charged with sustaining even the institutions of law and order in the narrow sense, but lawyers have a special responsibility in this connection. It is therefore important whether they appreciate the institutional dimension of what they are doing, merely administer the letter of the law, or introduce some special bias which is unrelated to the institutions they service. Not everyone can be an institutional liberal like the two judges whom I have quoted—or is that merely giving away my own kind of special bias?

There is much that could be said about the training and selection of lawyers, the social definition of their position, their relationship to other groups in society, their precarious independence. All this would end up with the search for one virtue which has much to do with institutions, the virtue of authority. Theodor Eschenburg resurrects the Latin word, *auctoritas*, but then distinguishes between "institutional" and "personal authority."[41] The former term is probably redundant; institutions carry within them the notion of legitimacy which is intended. But they have to be filled by personal authority which is a delicate balance of qualities of leadership, institutional sense and contact with those who are affected by decisions. "Only where these contacts exist but leadership remains in the lead, where it knows what needs to be done and works convincingly for its solutions, can one speak of authority in the democratic sense."[42] Eschenburg's advice to politicians holds *mutatis mutandis* for judges, police officers and all others with special responsibility for human affairs. Such personal authority too is an answer to the problem of law and order.

But the virtues required of all inhabitants of the institutional edifice are even more important. They take us one more time to the *homo sociologicus* syndrome. There are those who practice straightforward compliance with norms, whether thoughtless or fearful. They lack the imagination or the courage even to consider deviance. Needless to say, they are not the stuff from which the citizens of a free society are made. They leave norms without meaning and drain the lifeblood of institutions. But then there are those who have a peculiar sloppy attitude to norms. They recognise them for what they are, on the whole observe them, but leave no doubt in the minds of bystanders or those on whom the normative force of society is brought to bear, that if it was for them these norms would be quite different and might perhaps not exist at all. They are players of roles rather than actors who merge with their parts. Even while they apply sanctions—and this attitude is particularly frequent among administrators of many grades—they shrug their shoulders with a wry smile as if to say that they know fully well what nonsense they are doing, but it happens to be their job to do it. The result of this attitude is twofold. In practice, it does not lead to any changes of norms whether in the direction desired by those who apply them or any other direction. On the contrary, by their cynical application prevailing norms are confirmed to the point of ossification. So far as underlying attitudes are concerned on the other hand, the basis of legitimacy is pulled away from under the norms. Norms are separated from institutions, and the world that emerges combines formal compliance with a profound deprecation of all things social. Those who contribute to such a world are not the stuff either from which the citizens of a free society are made.

The institutional liberalism advocated here requires a different attitude. Fundamentally, this is certainly one of accepting society. More precisely, it is informed by a basic preparedness to regard the normative structure of society as home. But home is not just the place to live out one's more sociable inclinations; our unsociability too has its place in this structure. The basic inclination is merely the personal side of the social contract. It concerns fundamental institutional assumptions if and when these do not violate the first principles of the optimal state which we have discussed. The inclination extends in principle to specific norms. But here it has to be qualified. Either norms are acceptable in the full sense of being anchored in institutions, or they need to be changed to regain this quality. In both cases, they are taken seriously. The demand for change in particular is not an excuse for opting out, but a need for action in accordance with the groundrules which are themselves a part of any institutional arrangement. Liberty then is the insistent preservation of those institutions which offer citizenship, and the equally insistent battle for change in the interest of increasing life chances. But change means change of rules and through rules, whether its immediate objective is redistribution or institution-building, a minimum wage for all or the recovery of the "no-go area" of youth. The normative construction of society is neither a straitjacket nor a toy for essentially private players; it is the achievement of human ingenuity which provides us with coordinates of meaning and orientation, and also with the material to shape an even better future.

"Even better": there are assumptions here which need to be made explicit. In these lectures, we have assumed that the battle against authoritarian constraints has been won. One great historical transition has taken place if not once and for all—for that we can never know—then at least for the foreseeable future. It is the transition of modernity, and notably of its second stage, the Enlightenment and the French Revolution. Unquestioned ties, norms from which the privileged are excepted, the traditional legitimation of power are no longer the major issue to contend with if liberty is one's objective. There may be, and undoubtedly are, authoritarian corners left in all societies, but even in those which we sometimes describe as traditional, the presumption has come to be that mobilisation, participation, and an economic and social position which makes choices possible, are guiding values. Authoritarianism is dead, and the fact that some rearguard battles are still being fought, must not detract our attention.

Given modernity, the dangers to liberty are different. At many points in these lectures, we have identified two risks. To use current language, our opponents were not only the "dries" but also the "wets," or at any rate exaggerated versions of both. The "super-wets" are in fact false heralds of liberty. They glide along the greasy rails of fashion without realising that they have already passed their destination. This destination is also ours, in that sense they are friends. But all those catching, if not very beautiful words like democratisation, individualisation, communitarianism, and so on, have come to describe an attitude which helps weaken and ultimately erode social institutions. They tend towards a liberty without meaning, a freedom to choose without choices that make any sense. They serve to increase disorder, doubt and uncertainty for all. Those who follow this path run the risk which we have put in the phrase that people are seeking Rousseau but finding

Hobbes, and the risk is not just one for the seekers but for all who find themselves in their world. The false heralds of liberty are full of good intentions, but they pave a road which may lead if not to hell then to the nearest to it on earth, to Anomia.

This is a terribly foreshortened summary argument. In fact, we still have a long way to go on this road, even in the cities and countries in which law and order appear to be most threatened. Similarly, the "dry" or hard response to such modern trends is in practice rarely as serious as we have made it sound. But the response is strong. It is the view of those who say that the slide down the road to Anomia cannot go on, and that we have to reverse the trend. In economic and social policy, this involves a new social Darwinism according to which only the fittest have the right to survive. In the wider sphere of values, a resurrection of traditional values—we have called them, Victorian—is called for. In the narrower field in which we are above all interested the demand is for formal law and manifest order. And this is precisely the problem. From whatever angle we look at these reversers of the trend, they not only display little sense of history, but above all they lack understanding of the deeper forces of law and order, of institutions. Thus they naïvely take us back to some of the worst experiences of the age of class struggles; they reenact the class struggle from above; and they also saddle us with an aggravated version of the problem which they propose to solve. Not only social conditions, but hypernomia too, the multiplication of formal rules and sanctions without any anchor in institutions, lessens confidence in the social order. The new social contract remains a need, but one that is far from satisfied.

It is important to emphasise that both these opponents operate for the most part within the rules of the open society. One can challenge them by public debate and by canvassing political support for a different view. But it cannot have escaped anyone that underneath such a search for support there is a latent fear; apart from democratic opponents, a real enemy has accompanied our argument throughout. The enemy is, totalitarianism. Dismantling authoritarian structures was a secular process. It has revealed many ugly corners of abuse of privilege and the suppression of people. It has also involved many painful events, including revolutions and counter-revolutions. But in some way, and without wishing to use blanket terms to excuse human misery, the process made sense. It did lead to increasing human life chances. The catchwords of the French Revolution and even more so, the great hopes of the American Revolution, heralded progress. This is not the case when it comes to the great danger of our time, the totalitarian threat.

For a while I believed that we had reached the end of the age of totalitarianism. It seemed to me then that this age was a specific result of the faultings of old and new characteristic for example of Germany in the first half of this century, and perhaps (though this is less clear) of Russia a decade after the Revolution as well. I also thought that the Second World War, and the much underestimated Khruschev revelations after Stalin's death, had put an end to the horrible story which may have cost more than 50

million lives in Auschwitz and Gulag, on the battle-
fields and in the homes of East and West. It seemed
to me that the intellectual case for totalitarianism
had been settled once and for all by the great liberal
thinkers of the age, Karl Popper in their vanguard,
and also by those lesser if no less important writers
who belatedly came to recognize that their God had
failed.[43] I thought that we are moving into an age of
many uncertainties, but equipped with the framework and the memories which would enable us to
cope without new threats to liberty.

Today, I am no longer so sure. Not only do Pol Pot
and Amin and Duvalier, and even the tinpot dicta-
tors of the Mediterranean and of Latin America
make one wonder about the infectiousness of the
totalitarian virus, but there are questions nearer
home. One is what Fritz Stern calls "National Socialism as a temptation."[44] He is quite right to remind
us how many of the apparently good and great fell
for the new regime in 1933, and we know of course
how many fell vicariously at least for the terrors of
Stalinism. He points out also that there are promises
in these movements which appeal to disoriented and
uncertain people. For this is the other reason for my
new apprehension that the social condition and the
political background which may make totalitarian
answers attractive are still with us, and are perhaps
even more compelling than in the Weimar Republic
of Germany.

Franz Neumann gave his important book about
the "structure and practice of National Socialism" a
strange title when he called it, *Behemoth*.[45] Thomas
Hobbes had revived that land monster of the Old

Testament along with the sea monster, Leviathan. But Hobbes had used the name of Behemoth to describe the history of the civil war. Neumann knows that, of course, and points out himself that Hobbes described as Behemoth "an unstate, a chaos, a condition of lawlessness, of rebellion and of anarchy."[46] As a matter of fact, both Behemoth and Leviathan were monsters of chaos which is appropriate enough for in a sense one represents Anomia and the other, the reality of Utopia, tyranny. However that may be, rather curiously, Neumann then proceeds to describe the reality of National Socialism itself in the terms of Behemoth.[47] This requires involved turns of argument such as that National Socialist Germany not only had no political theory, but really no state either. I wish that had been true. In fact, the absolute, or rather total quality of the state (which Neumann knew and analysed so well) made it all too real, and the twisted political theory of exclusive citizenship served to "justify" the mass murder of Jews.

Alas it seems more appropriate to return to the original Behemoth of Hobbes. The absence of a credible state, lawlessness, the resulting mix of chaos and rebellion describe not totalitarianism, but the condition which gives rise to it. Some of its ingredients were clearly present in Weimar Germany, though in retrospect the 1920s look much less anomic than its contemporaries thought. Whether there were elements of anomy in the Soviet Union which Stalin inherited when he took over, or what other conditions enabled him to set up his murderous tyranny, is a question which I must leave open at this point. In any case, we have seen that Anomia cannot last. It is not just chaos, but also a vaccuum which attracts the most brutal forces and powers. We have also seen traces of such crude power and its arrogance in the contemporary world. Suffice it to say that my worry is that the road to Anomia will awaken Behemoth as well as Leviathan, and that a new wave of totalitarianism will sweep the world. The concern is not the least motive for these lectures. Berlin 1945 is after all not just a telling illustration of anomy, it is also the result of a process which began with anomic trends and totalitarian responses to it. It should not be forgotten that those images of Berlin with which I began are not merely a social model, but history, and an unforgettable memory of the link between abandoning liberty and abandoning all that is worthwhile in life.

At an early point, I have quoted the Weimar Chancellor Wirth with his statement that the enemy is on the right, and associated myself with it. To many, this may seem surprising. And in fact, in the normal course of the events of democratic political life, many irritants come from the left. Perhaps the left is there to irritate a cosy establishment of order and self-satisfaction. Such irritations are not always amusing. At one end of the spectrum, they include the revolutionary threat. But then, revolutions are rare. There are no more than a handful in any century. We still quote the great revolutions as landmarks of history. Among other things, revolutions are rare because they involve the many who on the whole, and except in most unusual circumstances, want their peace and quiet or rather, want to do their own things which has to do with life rather than with politics. For precisely this reason the many are, as long as the unusual does not happen, more inclined to give their support to those who demand quick action for the re-establishment of law and order, and who seek extraordinary powers to do what they want. The political right can count on a volume of built-in support which the left seeks forever in vain. Put in straight political terms, the wobbly centre is at the end of the day more readily prepared to give its reluctant support to a leader of the right than to one of the left. The right can win elections, even when the suspicion is abroad that it will begin its career in government with an "enabling law" which disables the rest, and is likely to end with terror and war. While it sets up its total grip on society, those whom we have called somewhat unkindly the wobbly centre, will probably stand around appeasing each other by saying that all this cannot last anyway and that the whole spook will soon be over. There were many who talked like this in Germany in 1933.

These lectures however are not a message of gloom. Their main thesis is another one: *tertium datur*. Once the open society has been closed, this is no longer the case. Under totalitarian rule, there are only two clear views, compliance or opposition. Everything else is at best self-delusion and at worst actual support for terror combined with irrelevant mental reservations. When the going gets rough for freedom, the choices are clear. But as long as the open society persists, there is a third approach which differs from both the wet democratic left and the dry democratic right (as well as variants of these combinations). We have called it, institutional liberalism.

Its two major tenets have to do with the two articles of the social contract which we have admitted. One is, the preservation of law and order as institutions rather than the mere surface of norms and sanctions. This requires holding on to what is valid, but more often, and especially today, it requires re-building and more, new construction. It is thus an active process rather than one of conservation by inaction. The other tenet is about citizenship. We have allowed this great force for progress to become an excuse for marginalisation and exclusion. This will not do. Economic and social policy can, and must still be informed by the search for the greatest life chances of all members of society, and that means, by citizenship for all. The majority class will have to give if it does not want to lose all, and this too is a task for those who want liberty above everything else. Law and order is the key.

Notes

1. The Road to Anomia

[1] *Cf.* C. Brinkmann, *Soziologie der Revolution* (Vandenhoeck & Ruprecht, Göttingen, 1948); pp. 48 *et seq.* The notion of the "paradox in the right of revolutions" is Nicolai Hartmann's.

[2] The (Catholic) Centre Party Chancellor Joseph Wirth ended his great *Reichstag* speech on Rathenau's murder in 1922 ("let us seek the path of freedom for our unhappy country in humility and patience") with the sentence: "The enemy stands where Mephisto drips his poison into the open wounds of a people, that is where the enemy stands, and there is no doubt about it: *dieser Feind steht rechts.*"

[3] *Cf.* K. Popper; *The Open Society and Its Enemies* (Routledge & Kegan Paul; London, 1952), vol. I, p. 201: "We must go on into the unknown, the uncertain and insecure, using what reason we may have to plan for both security *and* freedom."

[4] For the connection between anomy, civil war, revolution and law and order, see pp. 38 *et seq.*, below.

[5] For the "Hobbesian problem of order" see T. Parsons, *The Social System* (Free Press, Glencoe Ill, 1951), pp. 36 *et seq.*

[6] The (German) magazine is called *Berlins feine Adressen*, and the Editorial by E. O. Schwarzer is from the February 1985 issue.

[7] Reported by C. E. Silberman, *Criminal Violence, Criminal Justice* (Random House, New York, 1978), p. 6.

[8] R. Nozick, *Anarchy, State and Utopia* (Blackwell, Oxford, 1974).

[9] Comparative evidence up to the early 1970s has been gathered by

D. Archer and R. Gartner, *Violent Crime in Cross-National Perspective* (Yale University Press, New Haven-London, 1984).

[10] L. Radzinowicz and J. King, *The Growth of Crime* (Penguin Books, Harmondsworth, 19079), p. 59.

[11] *Op. cit.*, p. 24.

[12] "Victimology" has become a science in its own right. *Cf., e.g.* the five volumes edited by I. Drapkin and E. Viamo *Victimology: a New Focus* (D. C. Health, Lexington, 1970)

[13] M. Zander, "What Is the Evidence on Law and Order?" *New Society*, vol. 50 no. 897 (December 13, 1979), p. 591.

[14] L. McDonald, *The Sociology of Law and Order* (Book Center, Montreal, 1976), p. 13.

[15] J. Q. Wilson, "Crime in the Streets" in *Law and Order in a Democratic Society* (M. R. Summers and T. E. Barth eds, Charles E. Merrill, Columbus, 1970). the quotation is on p. 8.

[16] D. Downes, *Law and Order: Theft of an Issue* (Fabian Tract 490, Blackrose Press, London, 1983), p. 8. The "adage" was of course the title of a play by Franz Werfel: *Nicht der Mörder, sondern der Ermordete ist schuldig.*

[17] This is suggested by D. Archer and R. Gartner: *op. cit.* p. 3 and appendices.

[18] D. Archer and R. Gartner conclude that "wars do tend to legitimate the general use of violence in domestic society" (*op. cit.*, p. 92).

[19] E. H. Powell: "Crime as a Function of Anomie" in *Law and Order in a Democratic Society* (M. R. Summers and T. E. Barth eds, Charles E. Merrill, Columbus, 1970), p. 28. With respect to the Civil War, Powell reports his own study of "The Crime Trend in Buffalo, New York 1854–1956"; for the "First American Revolution" he quotes the book by C. Briedenbaugh, *Cities in Revolt: Urban Life in America 1743–1776. Cf.* in this connection also L. Radzinowicz and J. King, "A longer view, peering into the middle ages, or even the eighteenth century, might well give more substance to the theory [of growing violence]. With all our crime, our society is more secure, less savage than theirs. But there are no statistics to guide us there" (*op. cit.* p. 23).

[20] B. Tuchman, *A Distant Mirror. The Calamitous 14th Century* (A. Knopf, New York, 1978).

[21] B. Tuchman, *op. cit.* p. 581.

[22] I. Deane Jones, *The English Revolution* (Heinemann, London, 1931), p. 323. See also the preceding sentence: "It was only when war had shattered the traditional organisation of society that men began to ask fundamental questions about the nature and purposes of government; Englishmen became political theorists because the urgent task of reconstruction after 1645 compelled them to adopt some general principles, old or new, to help them in the task."

[23] Quoted in R. Mischke, "Wir lachen sie kaputt," *Frankfurter Allgemeine Zeitung*, March 9, 1985.

[24] L. Radzinowicz and J. King, *op. cit.*, p. 63.

[25] D. Downes, *op. cit.* p. 12.

[26] The book in question is H. Popitz, *Die normative Konstruktion von Gesellschaft* (Mohr/Siebeck, Tübingen, 1980). The "little piece" is called, in the original: *Über die Präventivwirkung des Nichtwissens* (Recht und Staat 350, Mohr/Siebeck, Tübingen, 1968).

[27] H. Popitz, *op. cit.*, p. 9.

[28] H. Popitz, *op. cit.*, p. 12.

[29] *Cf.* C. M. Glennie, "Crime in England and Wales" *Social Trends* No. 7 (HMSO, London, 1976), p. 36.

[30] For example by M. Hough and P. Mayhew, *The British Crime Survey—First Report* (Home Office Research Study 76, HMSO, London, 1983).

[31] Thus in *Compact Edition of the Oxford English Dictionary* (Oxford University Press, Oxford, 1971).

[32] This is Popitz's term in *Die normative Konstruktion*, etc. *op. cit.* p. 65. The word is hard to translate, because *Verzicht* entails both a subjective (withholding) and an objective (exemption) element; waiver is probably closest. Popitz himself tends to underestimate the usefulness of the term which he calls, a "residual category."

[33] H. Popitz, *Über die Präventivwirkung*, etc., p. 13.

[34] E. Durkheim, *Suicide* (Free Press, Glencoe Ill., 1951), p. 252

[35] L. McDonald, *op. cit.*, p. 103.

[36] J. Baechler, *Les suicides* (Calmann-Levy, Paris, 1975) pp. 99, 449.

[37] L. Radzinowicz and J. King, *op. cit.*, p. 94.

[38] This is an allusion to a statement by R. M. MacIver, *The Ramparts We Guard* (Macmillan, New York, 1950), pp. 84 *et seq.* The statement has been interpreted by R. K. Merton (see n. 39) and in my *Life Chances* (Weidenfeld and Nicolson, London, 1979), and is sufficiently important to be quoted in full: "Anomy signifies the state of mind of one who has been pulled up by his moral roots, who has no longer any standards, but only disconnected urges, who has no longer any sense of continuity of folk, of obligation. The anomic man has become spiritually sterile, responsive only to himself, responsible to no one. He derides the values of other men. His only faith is the philosophy of denial. He lives on the thin line of sensation between no future and no past. . . . Anomy is a state of mind in which the individual's sense of social cohesion—the mainspring of his morale—is broken or fatally weakened."

[39] The two essays are of course, "Social Structure and Anomie" and "Continuities in the Theory of Social Structure and Anomie." Both are contained in R. K. Merton, *Social Theory and Social Structure* (Rev. Ed., Free Press, Glencoe Ill., 1957). The quotation is on p. 162.

[40] A. Giddens, "A Typology of Suicide" *European Journal of Sociology*, vol. vii, no. 2 (1966) pp. 290 *et seq.*

[41] This is very close to H. Popitz, *Die normative Konstruktion*, etc., *loc. cit.* who in turn follows T. Geiger, *Vorstudien zu einer Soziologie des Rechts* (E. Munksgaard, Copenhagen, 1947).

[42] E. Durkheim, *op. cit.*, p. 252.

[43] R. K. Merton, *op. cit.*, p. 157.

[44] Hence my polemical essay: "Out of Utopia" reprinted in *Essays in the Theory of Society* (Stanford University Press, Stanford, 1968).

[45] M. Zander, *op. cit.*, p. 593.

[46] M. Streck, "Der Steuerhinterzieher als Mandant" in *Betriebs-Berater*, vol. 39, no. 35/36 (December 1984).

[47] *Cf.* L. Radzinowicz and J. King, *op. cit*, pp. 35, 29 and C. E. Silberman: *op. cit.*, p. 31.

[48] *Cf.* The chapter on "Law Enforcement" in *Social Trends* No. 10 (HMSO: London, 1980).

[49] In the case of Mr. Goetz to which this statement alludes, the Grand Jury had second thoughts after evidence about his motives had come to light.

[50] M. Weber, *Wirtschaft und Gesellschaft* (4th ed., Mohr/Siebeck, Tübingen, 1956), §17.

[51] R. M. Momboisse, *Riots, Revolts and Insurrections* (C. C. Thomas: Springfield Ill., 1967) p. 442. The "manual" contains plausible descriptions of the emergence of riots and revolts.

[52] The event in question occurred on the occasion of the Luton-Millwall game on March 14, 1985. Its significance is in the fact that it led the Prime Minister to demand harsher sanctions and may thus provide additional material about techniques of riot control as well as the readiness of all involved to enforce norms.

[53] *The Brixton Disorders 10–12 April 1981*, Report of an Inquiry by Lord Scarman (HMSO, London, 1981), p. 42.

[54] Quoted by Lord Scarman *loc. cit.* from *Halsbury's Laws of England.*

[55] *Report of the National Advisory Commission on Civil Disorders*, March 1968 (Chairman: O. Kerner). For Lord Scarman's report, see n. 53.

[56] Thus in W. Sombart: *Why Is There No Socialism in the United States?* (Macmillan, London-Basingstoke, 1976). The book was originally published in 1906.

[57] Marx regarded "competition between individuals" as a preliminary phase of conflict, to be followed by the organised class struggle. Thus in the first part of the *Communist Manifesto*: "The organisation of proletarians as a class, and thus a political party, is disrupted all the time by competition among the workers themselves. . . . "

2. Seeking Rousseau, Finding Hobbes

[1] This is of course taken from the first sentence of Chap. 1 of Rousseau's *Contrat Social*.

[2] Kant's little essay, "Beantwortung der Frage: Was ist Aufklärung?" ("Response to the Question: What Is Englightenment?"), first published in 1784 (and included in most collections of his essays) begins with the sentence: "*Aufklärung ist der Ausgang des Menschen aus seiner selbst verschuldeten Unmündigkeit.*"

[3] L. Radzinowicz and J. King, *The Growth of Crime* (Penguin Books, Harmondsworth, 1979), p. 134.

[4] I have first used the term, ligatures, extensively in my book *Life Chances* (Weidenfeld & Nicolson, London, 1981), Chaps. 2 and 3. The term, derived from the Latin verb, *ligare*, has both the advantage and the disadvantage of being "artificial." Evidently, it is close to Durkeim's "bonds" (as well as his notion of "solidarity") and similar notions elsewhere.

[5] These references not only refer explicitly to J. P. Sartre's play, *La Nausée*, but also to his concept of "total freedom" ("without call, without shadow, without past, merely an invisible tearing-oneself-away into the future") and the consequent notion of pure action. E. Mounier, in his *Introduction aux existentialismes* (Denoel, Paris, 1951), Chap. vi is not the only one to take Sartre to task for not having "an idea of man revealed in history, but transcending history."

[6] W. Maihofer, "Menschenbild und Strafrechtsreform" in *Gesellschaftliche Wirklichkeit im 20. Jahrhundert und Strafrechtsreform* (FU Berlin, Universitätstage 1964, W. de Gruyter, Berlin, 1964), p. 5. Some of the "alternative professors" (including Maihofer) are represented with their own contributions in *Die deutsche Strafrechtsreform* (L. Reinisch ed., C. H. Beck, Munich, 1967). Maihofer later became the "chief ideologist" of the Free Democratic Party and, from 1974 to 1978, Federal Minister of Interior.

[7] W. Maihofer, *op. cit.*, pp. 6, 8, 12.

[8] W. Maihofer, *op. cit.*, p. 14. The suspicious phrase, "also . . . equally more or less exclusively" is in the original text.

[9] W. Maihofer, *op. cit.*, pp. 17, 18.

[10] W. Maihofer, *op. cit.*, p. 22.

[11] W. Maihofer, *op. cit.*, p. 23.

[12] Virtually all the authors quoted in the first lecture—D. Archer and R. Gartner, C. Silberman, D. Downes, L. McDonald, the contributors to the volume edited by M. R. Summers and T. E. Barth—subscribe to this view. My selection—or the sign of a prevailing view?

[13] J. Habermas, *Theorie des kommunikativen Handelns* (Suhrkamp,

Frankfurt, 1981), vol. ii, p. 520. The following quotations are all from vol. ii.

[14] J. Habermas, *op. cit.*, p. 526. The English word, civil society, loses of course half the meaning of the German, *bürgerliche Gesellschaft*, which signifies both "civil" and "bourgeois" society. When Habermas speaks of the "system perspective," he is using the terminology mentioned in the first lecture ("social integration," "system integration" see p. 22 above).

[15] J. Habermas, *op. cit.*, p. 481.

[16] J. Habermas, *op. cit.*, p. 223.

[17] J. Habermas, *op. cit.*, pp. 223 *et seq.*

[18] J. Habermas, *op. cit.*, p. 286.

[19] J. Habermas, *op. cit.*, p. 518.

[20] J. Habermas, *Legitimitätsprobleme im Spätkapitalismus* (Suhrkamp, Frankfurt, 1973), p. 125.

[21] J. Habermas, *Legitimationsprobleme*, etc., p. 144.

[22] J.-J. Rousseau, *Du contrat social*, Book i, Chap. vi. Quoted from the edition by M. Touquet (Baudouin Frères, Paris s.d.).

[23] G. W. F. Hegel, *Grundlinien der Philosophie des Rechts*, (J. Hoffmeister ed., F. Meiner, Hamburg, 1955), §258.

[24] J.-J. Rousseau, *Émile*, transl. by B. Foxley (Dent, London, 1974).

[25] J.-J. Rousseau, *op. cit.*, p. 30.

[26] J.-J. Rousseau, *op. cit.*, pp. 42 *et seq.*

[27] J.-J. Rousseau, *op. cit.*, p. 53.

[28] J.-J. Rousseau, *op. cit.*, p. 125.

[29] J.-J. Rousseau, *op. cit.*, p. 182.

[30] J.-J. Rousseau, *op. cit.*, p. 198.

[31] J.-J. Rousseau, *op. cit.*, p. 204.

[32] J.-J. Rousseau, *op. cit.*, p. 211.

[33] J.-J. Rousseau, *op. cit.*, p. 216.

[34] J.-J. Rousseau, *op. cit.*, p. 256.

[35] J.-J. Rousseau, *op. cit.*, p. 274.

[36] J.-J. Rousseau, *op. cit.*, p. 299.

[37] J.-J. Rousseau, *op. cit.*, p. 436.

[38] J.-J. Rousseau, *op. cit.*, p. 357.

[39] J.-J. Rousseau, *op. cit.*, p. 370.

[40] J.-J. Rousseau, *op. cit.*, pp. 442 *et seq.*

[41] J.-J. Rousseau, *op. cit.*, p. 280.

[42] Terms used by R. K. Merton in his "typology of modes of individual adaptation" on p. 140 of "Social Structure and Anomie" in *Social Theory and Social Structure* (Rev. ed., Free Press, Glencoe Ill., 1957).

[43] M. Stirner, *Der Einzige und sein Eigentum* (D. Wigand, Leipzig, 1845).

[44] J. Joll, *The Anarchists* (2nd ed., Methuen, London, 1979), p. 16.

[45] J. L. Talmon, *The Origins of Totalitarian Democracy* (Mercury Books, London, 1961), Chap. iii. At this point at the latest one friend who may feel upset about this lecture would argue that my critique is not of Rousseau, but of Rousseau as misunderstood in Germany. There undoubtedly are "latter-day German adepts of an already Germanified [*eingedeutscht*] Rousseau" (thus K. H. Bohrer, "Die Unschuld an die Macht" in *Merkur* January/1985); but it is hard to see how one could interpret Rousseau differently from the attempt made here.

[46] J. L. Talmon, *op. cit.*, p. 39.

[47] *Cf.* E. Mounier (n. 5, above): "Heavy-handed polemics have tried to relate Sartre's philosophy to National Socialism. We do not want to leave the shadow of a doubt that we will have no part of such tendentious claims. . . . "

[48] Peachum's refrain somehow sounds more impressive in German: "*Doch die Verhältnisse, die sind nicht so.*"

[49] T. Hobbes, *Leviathan*, ed. A. D. Lindsay (Dent, London, 1914) pp. 64 *et seq.*

[50] J. Alderson, *Law and Disorder* (Hamish Hamilton, London, 1984), p. 215. In the early chapter on "Social Order and Disorder" Alderson actually seems to subscribe to a Hobbesian view of man, but the more practical his book becomes, the closer its author gets to Rousseau.

[51] J. Alderson, *op. cit.*, pp. 215 *et seq.*

[52] A. Gehlen, "Das Bild des Menschen im Lichte der modernen Anthropologie" *Philosophische Anthropologie und Handlungslehre* (Collected Works, vol. 4, Vittorio Klostermann, Frankfurt, 1983) pp. 132 *et seq.*

[53] I. Kant, "Idee zu einer allgemeinen Geschichte in weltbürgerlicher Absicht" in *Kants Populäre Schriften* (P. Menzer ed., Georg Reimer, Berlin, 1911).

[54] K. R. Popper, *The Open Society and its Enemies* (Routledge & Kegan Paul, London, 1952), vol. ii, pp. 269 *et seq.*

[55] I. Kant, *op. cit.* All quotations in this paragraph are from the "Fourth Statement" (*Vierter Satz*).

[56] I. Kant, *op. cit.* All quotations in this paragraph are from the "Fifth Statement" (*Fünfter Satz*).

[57] The long article on "Hobbisme ou Philosophie de Hobbes" is here quoted from the 1782 edition of the *Encyclopédie* (Societés Typographiques, Lausanne & Berne), p. 588. The author even ventures into a biographical explanation of the differences: "One [Hobbes] was born in the middle of tumultousness and factional strife; the other lived in the social world and among scholars. Different times, different circumstances, a different philosophy."

[58] D. Hume, *A Treatise of Human Nature*, ed. L. A. Selby-Bigge (Clarendon Press, Oxford, 1888) pp. 486 *et seq.*

[59] J. Locke, *The Second Treatise of Government*, ed. T. P. Peardon (Liberal Arts Press, New York, 1952), p. 14.

[60] K. R. Popper, *op. cit.*, vol. i, pp. 200 *et seq.*

[61] W. Maihofer, *Vom Sinn menschlicher Ordnung* (Vittorio Klostermann, Frankfurt, 1956). In this little treatise, Maihofer begins with Kant's demand to "be general," *i.e.* to consider acts as if they were to be general norms, goes on to Nietzsche's demand to "be thyself," and ends up developing what with a Heideggerianism he calls the *Selbstsein im Alssein*, *i.e.* being oneself by playing social roles.

[62] One rather persuasive example is J. Baumann (another "alternative professor"!): *Beschränkung des Lebensstandards anstatt kurzfristiger Freiheitsstrafe* (Luchterhand, Neuwied-Berlin, 1968). See also the balanced discussion of "Sentencing" in L. Radzinowicz and J. King, *op. cit.*, Chap. 8.

[63] J. Baumann, *op. cit.*

[64] The subject of the limitations of the law is ancient; although with respect to its specific formulation suggested here, F. von Hayek is undoubtedly right: "The relation between the character of the legal order and the functioning of the market system has received comparatively little study, and most of the work in this field has been done by men who were critical of the competitive order rather than by its supporters." See *The Constitution of Liberty* (Routledge & Kegan Paul, London, 1960), p. 229. Hayek's work offers many a liberal insight into the relation between law and economics. *Cf.* also his *Law, Legislation and Liberty* (Univeristy of Chicago Press, Chicago, 1973–1979).

[65] D. Bell, "The Return of the Sacred?" in *The Winding Passage* (Abt Books, Cambridge, Mass., 1980). *Cf.* P. Rieff, *Triumph of the Therapeutic* (Harper & Row, New York, 1966).

[66] Of Küng's major works on the subject, one is the book of the priest: *Christ sein* (Piper, Münich, 1974), transl. as *On Being a Christian*; the other is the book of the shcolar: *Existiert Gott?* (Piper, Munich, 1978) transl. *Does God Exist?* More recently, Küng has tempered his Christianity by a more ecumenical approach; *cf.* H. Küng *et al.*, *Christentum und Weltreligionen* (Piper, Munich, 1984). Needless to say, this brief reference does less than justice to a great project of analysis and of theory.

[67] H. Küng, *Christ sein, loc. cit.*, p. 366.

[68] H. Küng, *Existiert Gott?, loc. cit.*, p. 484.

[69] H. Albert, *Das Elend der Theologie* (Hoffmann & Campe, Hamburg, 1979), p. 76.

[70] J. Baechler, "Mourir a Jonestown" in (1979) *European Journal of Sociology*, vol. xx, no. 2.

[71] E. F. Schumacher, *Small Is Beautiful* (Blond & Briggs, London, 1973), p. 17.

[72] *Cf.* J. Alderson, *op. cit.*

[73] J. Strasser, *Grenzen des Sozialstaats?* (Europäische Verlagsanstalt, Cologne-Frankfurt, 1979), p. 113 *et passim*. Naturally, or so one is tempted to say, Strasser uses the word, *gemeinschaftlich* and thus revives Tönnies's old contrast of *Gemeinschaft* and *Gesellschaft*.

[74] *Cf.* J. Habermas, "Die neue Unübersichtlichkeit" in *Merkur*, vol. xxxix, no. 1 (January 1985).

[75] The books cited in this paragraph are, in this sequence: D. H. Meadows *et al.*, *The Limits to Growth* (A Report to the Club of Rome, Universe Books, New York, 1972). J. W. Botkin *et al.*, *No Limits to Learning* (A Report to the Club of Rome, Pergamon Press, Oxford, 1979). E. F. Schumacher, *op. cit.* E. Mishan, *The Economic Growth Debate* (Allen & Unwin, London, 1977). F. Hirsch, *Social Limits to Growth* (Routledge & Kegan Paul, London, 1977). L. R. Brown, *Building a Sustainable Society* (Norton & Co., New York-London, 1981). E. Eppler, *Wege aus der Gefahr* (Rowohlt, Hamburg, 1981). A. H. Halsey, *Change in British Society* (Oxford University Press, Oxford, 1978). The selection is almost random; a score of other authors could easily be added to this list of economists and other social scientists who have become promoters of ethics by the force of things.

[76] *Tendenzwende* is the German word for this process, and the book under that title (Ernst Klett, Stuttgart, 1975) assembles many of the authors one would expect to find. It includes a piece of mine on ligatures, which shows how hard it is in this field to keep the right company.

[77] Their theorists can for the most part be found among the authors of the magazine, *Commentary*.

[78] F. Stern's important book has never lost its topicality, at any rate for Germany: *The Politics of Cultural Despair* (University of California Press, Berkeley-Los Angeles, 1961).

[79] C. E. Silberman, *Criminal Violence, Criminal Justice* (Random House, New York, 1978), pp. 428 *et seq.*

3. The Struggle for the Social Contract

[1] S. M. Lipset, *Political Man* (Doubleday, Garden City, 1960), Chaps. vii and viii. The expression is borrowed from D. Anderson and P. Davidson, *Ballots and the Democratic Class Struggle* (Stanford University Press, Stanford, 1943).

[2] S. M. Lipset, *op. cit.*, p. 220.

[3] This is a play on the German words *Not* and *Notwendigkeit* which leads Marx to the mistaken belief that extreme deprivation makes the revolution inevitable. *Cf.* "Die Heilige Familie" in *MEGA* I, 3, p. 368.

[4] Even in England, the amazing "decline of the industrial spirit"

would not have been possible without the survival of the values of a pre-industrial aristocracy. *Cf.* M. Wiener, *English Culture and the Decline of the Industrial Spirit 1850–1980* (Cambridge University Press, Cambridge, 1981).

⁵ The levelling of skills is a persistent theme of the early political economists and Marx which I have analysed, and refuted in my (unpublished London Ph.D. thesis of 1956) *Unskilled Labour in British Industry*.

⁶ W. Sombart, *Why Is There No Socialism in the United States?* (Macmillan London-Basingstoke, 1976). T. Veblen, *Imperial Germany and the Industrial Revolution* (Viking Press, New York, 1939). Sombart's book was first published in 1906, Veblen's in 1915.

⁷ T. Geiger, *Die Klassengesellschaft im Schmelztiegel* (G. Kiepenheuer, Cologne-Hagen, 1949) pp. 182 *et seq.*

⁸ T. H. Marshall, *Citizenship and Social Class* (Cambridge University Press, Cambridge, 1950).

⁹ T. H. Marshall, *op. cit.*, pp. 46–47.

¹⁰ K. Middlemas, *Politics in Industrial Society* (A. Deutsch, London, 1979).

¹¹ This is an allusion to G. Dangerfield, *The Strange Death of Liberal England* (Capricorn Books, New York, 1961).

¹² *Cf.* J. Schumpeter, *Capitalism, Socialism and Democracy* (Allen & Unwin, London, 1943), Chap. xxii. K. Arrow, *Social Choice and Individual Values* (John Wiley, New York, 1951). See also n. 21, below.

¹³ J. W. Gough, *The Social Contract* (2nd ed., Clarendon Press, Oxford, 1957) p. 1. This study continues to be instructive on the history of the concept and I have relied heavily on it.

¹⁴ *Cf.* p. 25, above.

¹⁵ 1889 was not only the year of publication of the *Fabian Essays*, but also that of the formation of the great trades' unions of the unskilled, and thus the end of "guerilla warfare." The point about the United States (see n. 6 above) or about 1919 hardly needs explanation.

¹⁶ *Cf.* Kant's "Idea for a General History," etc. quoted extensively in the second lecture (n. 53 in the notes to Chap. 2). My italics.

¹⁷ *Cf.* P. Bauer, "Class on the Brain" in *Equality, the Third World, and Economic Delusion* (Weidenfeld & Nicolson, London, 1981).

¹⁸ *Cf.* T. Geiger, *Die soziale Schichtung des deutschen Volkes* (F. Enke, Stuttgart, 1932) pp. 97 *et seq.* See also n. 46, below.

¹⁹ W. Sombart, *op. cit.*

²⁰ This point is developed in my *Conflict After Class* (Longmans for the University of Essex, London-Colchester, 1967).

²¹ A. Downs, *An Economic Theory of Democracy* (Harper & Brothers, New York, 1957).

[22] On the "end of ideology," *cf.* C. J. Waxman, *The "End of Ideology" Debate* (Funk & Wagnall, New York, 1968).

[23] This is an important point which is impressivley documented by P. Flora and A. J. Heidenheimen, *The Development of Welfare States in Europe and America* (Transaction Books, New Brunswick-London, 1981). See also J. Alber: *Vom Armenhaus zum Wohlfahrtsstaat* (Campus, Frankfurt-New York, 1982).

[24] Max Weber's analysis of bureaucracy is pertinent throughout this lecture. *Cf.* "Parlament und Regierung im neugeordneten Deutschland," in *Gesammelte Politische Schriften* (Mohr/Siebeck, Tübingen, 1958), p. 320.

[25] W. Dettling *et al.*, *Die neue soziale Frage und die Zukunft der Demokratie* (Eichholz Verlag, Bonn, 1976), p. 83. It is worth noting that this publication assembles authors close to the Christian Democratic Union (C.D.U).

[26] This may be more true in Germany than in Britain. *Cf.* the Report by *Der Spiegel*, vol. 38, no. 52, December 12, 1984 ("Kein Geld, kein Spass, wozu noch leben?").

[27] F. Field, *Inequality in Britain* (Fontana Paperbacks, Collins, Glasgow, 1981), pp. 49 *et seq.*

[28] M. Miegel, " 'Neue Armut': Die Regierung und die Tarifparteien tragen schwere Verantwortung für die Reform des Arbeitsmarktes" *Handelsblatt* No. 223, November 30, 1984. This author who has published widely on the subject, is also associated with the C.D.U.

[29] For some of this debate see the volume *Poverty and Inequality in Common Market Countries*, ed. by V. George and R. Lawson (Routledge & Kegan Paul, London, 1980). In this volume, the relevant figures are also given.

[30] K. Marx and F. Engels: *Manifesto of the Communist Party*, Pt. i.

[31] Many economists have come to assume a "natural rate of unemployment" of 7 or 8 per cent.

[32] The term was probably intorduced by the secretary general of the German Social Democratic Party (S.P.D.), Peter Glotz. *Cf.* his speech, "Ausgrenzung in die neue Armut" put out by the S.P.D. Press Service on December 5, 1984.

[33] *The Brixton Disorders*, Report of an Inquiry by Lord Scarman (HMSO, London, 1981), Pt. vi.

[34] C. E. Silberman, *Criminal Violence, Criminal Justice* (Random House, New York, 1978), p. 32.

[35] I owe this idea to T. Philips who has written about it for the volume by D. Steel, *Britain 2000* (Bodley Head, London, 1985).

[36] K. Marx and F. Engels, *loc. cit.*

[37] T. Geiger, *Die soziale Schichtung*, etc. *loc. cit.*, p. 91.

[38] T. Geiger, *Die soziale Schichtung*, etc. *loc. cit.*, p. 111.

[39] Reported by J. Seabrook, "The society which offers hope on the under-world lottery" in *The Guardian*, March 25, 1985.

[40] *Cf.* J. Habermas, *Legitimitätsprobleme im Spätkapitalismus* (Suhrkamp, Frankfurt, 1973), p. 68.

[41] M. Olson, *The Rise and Decline of Nations* (Yale University Press, New Haven-London, 1982), p. 203.

[42] M. Olson, *op. cit.*, p. 145.

[43] M. Weber, *op. cit.*, pp. 321 *et seq.*

[44] M. Miegel, *op. cit.*

[45] E. Lederer and J. Marschak, "Der neue Mittelstand" in *Grundriss der Sozialökonomik*, vol. ix/i (Mohr, Tübingen, 1926).

[46] *Cf.* K. Renner, *Wandlungen der modernen Gesellschaft* (Wiener Volksbuchhandlung, Vienna, 1953). J. Burnham, *The Managerial Revolution* (J. Day, New York, 1941). P. Bourdieu und J.-C. Passeron, *La Reproduction* (Ed. de Minuit: Paris 1970).

[47] D. Bell, *The Coming of Post-Industrial Society* (Basic Books, New York, 1973).

[48] D. Bell, *op. cit.*, p. 44.

[49] D. Bell, *op. cit.*, p. 378.

[50] R. Hofstadter, *Social Darwinism in American Thought*, (Rev. ed. Beacon Press, Boston, 1955), p. 6. Hofstadter identified the former view with William Graham Sumner, the latter with Herbert Spencer.

[51] R. Hofstadter, *op. cit.*, p. 8.

[52] *Scala mobile* is of course the Italian name for indexing wages and salaries.

[53] This is in fact the thesis of Marx's *18th Brumaire of Louis Bonaparte* in relation to the small-lot farmers who could not represent themselves and therefore had to be represented.

[54] *Cf.* I. Gilmour, *Inside Right* (Quarter Books, London, 1978).

[55] In *The Human Condition* (Doubleday, Garden City, 1959) H. Arendt uses the phrase in connection with her distinction between "labour," "work" and "action."

[56] "Theft of an issue" is the subtitle of D. Downes, *Law and Order* (Fabian Tract 490, Blackrose Press, London, 1983). See also I. Taylor, *Law and Order—Arguments for Socialism* (Macmillan, London-Basingstoke, 1981).

4. Society and Liberty

[1] W. Maihofer, *Vom Sinn menschlicher Ordung* (Vittorio Klostermann, Frankfurt, 1956), p. 64.

[2] J. Locke, *The Second Treatise of Government*, (T. P. Peardon ed., Liberal Arts Press, New York, 1952), p. 49.

³ A. Gehlen, *Philosophische Anthropologie und Handlungslehre* (Collected Works, vol. 4, Vittorio Klostermann, Frankfurt, 1983), p. 378.

⁴ A. Gehlen, *op. cit.*, p. 244.

⁵ J. Locke, *op. cit.*, p. 8.

⁶ J. Locke, *op. cit.*, p. 20.

⁷ The reference is to C. L. de Montesquieu's *L'esprit de lois*.

⁸ "Homo Sociologicus" is included in my *Essays in the Theory of Society* (Stanford University Press, Stanford, 1968). The quotation is on p. 87, and the reference to the "inhabitant of the earth" and the "inhabitant of a country" is to Robert Musil.

⁹ Thus Helmut Schelsky. For the quotation and my response in 1962, see "Sociology and Human Nature" in *Essays* etc. *loc. cit.*, p. 100.

¹⁰ Again, the discussion is in "Sociology and Human Nature" in *Essays*, etc. *loc. cit.*, pp. 108 *et seq.*

¹¹ The reference is to the discussion of Maihofer on pp. 46 *et seq.*, see also nn. 6, 61 in the notes to Chap. 2.

¹² J. Locke, *op. cit.*, p. 9.

¹³ D. Archer and R. Gartner, *Violent Crime in Cross-National Perspective* (Yale University Press, New York-London, 1984), p. 136.

¹⁴ The authors whom we have quoted throughout for their balanced views would agree. *Cf.* L. Radzinowicz and J. King, *The Growth of Crime* (Penguin Books, Harmondsworth, 1979), Chap. 9. C. E. Silberman, *Criminal Violence, Criminal Justice* (Random House, New York, 1978); Chaps. 6, 10.

¹⁵ This was the 1973 Standards and Goals Commission. *Cf.* C. E. Silberman, *op. cit.*, p. 371.

¹⁶ This is a reference to J. Baumann's book; *cf.* p. 68 above.

¹⁷ The friend is Walter Jens. The name of the *Amtsrichter* in question is Werner Offenloch. The text of his opinion was published by *Frankfurter Allgemeine Zeitung* on February 1, 1985 ("Sie sollten auch das in Ihre Sorge aufnehmen . . . ").

¹⁸ K. Mannheim, *Ideology and Utopie* (Routledge & Kegan Paul, London, 1968).

¹⁹ Thus T. Sellin in his Foreword to G. Rusche and O. Kirchheimer, *Punishment and Social Structure* (Russell & Russell, New York, 1967).

²⁰ G. Rusche and O. Kirchheimer, *op. cit.*, p. 207.

²¹ Thus on pp. 28 *et seq.* above.

²² *Cf.* J.-F. Revel, *Comment les démocraties finissent* (B. Grasset, Paris, 1983). See also J. Baechler, *Démocraties* (Calmann-Levy, Paris, 1985).

²³ M. Weber, "Parlament und Regierung im neugeordneten Deutschland" in *Politische Schriften* (Mohr/Siebeck, Tübingen, 1958).

²⁴ Thus J. Alderson, *Law and Disorder* (Hamish Hamilton, London, 1984), p. 194 and Chap. 13. In fairness, it should be added that Alder-

son's book also contains much material compatible with the proposals made in the following paragraph.

[25] The list is taken from an unpublished Ford Foundation document entitled *Neighborhood Security and Crime Prevention* (June 1982), *cf.* p. 10.

[26] Quoted in *The Brixton Disorders*, Report of an Inquiry by Lord Scarman (HMSO, London, 1981), p. 98.

[27] *Op. cit.* pp. 97 *et seq.*

[28] The former is a conservative, the latter a socialist fallacy: another reason for the "third way" advocated here.

[29] See p. 71 above.

[30] R. Nozick, *Anarchy State, and Utopia* (Basil Blackwell, Oxford, 1974) p. 4.

[31] R. Nozick, *op. cit.*, p. 23.

[32] R. Nozick, *op. cit.*, p. ix.

[33] R. Nozick, *op. cit.*, p. 334.

[34] Nozick rejects the Hobbesian state of nature, because as the "worst case" it also gives rise to the worst case of the state; see *op. cit.*, pp. 4 *et seq.*

[35] *Cf.* H. L. A. Hart, *The Concept of Law* (Clarendon Press, Oxford, 1961) and J. Rawls, *A Thoery of Justice* (Oxford University Press, London-Oxford, 1972). Rawls explicitly says (at p. 7) that "the primary subject of justice is the basic structure of society, or more exactly, the way in which the major social institutions distribute fundamental rights and duties and determine the division of advantages from social cooperation." The following sentence is also relevant in our context: "By major institutions I understand the political constitution and the principle economic and social arrangements."

[36] R. Nozick, *op. cit.*, p. 195.

[37] R. Nozick, *op. cit.*, p. 238.

[38] In the "Preface" to his book, Nozick discusses his own conversion from the views which his friends still hold.

[39] R. Nozick, *op. cit.*, p. 334. Nozick would probably underline the first part of this laconic conclusion; we would underline the second.

[40] W. Weyrauch, *The Personality of Lawyers* (Yale Unversity Press, New Haven-London, 1964). J. Griffith, *The Politics of the Judiciary* (Fontana Paperbacks, Glasgow, 1977). These are two of a long list of studies of the social origin and political bias of judges and lawyers more generally.

[41] T. Eschenburg, *Über Autorität* (Suhrkamp, Frankfurt, 1965). See especially the chapter on "authority in democracies," pp. 168 *et seq.*

[42] T. Eschenburg, *op. cit.*, p. 178.

[43] Hannah Arendt and Friedrich von Hayek, but also Alexander Solzhenitsyn and many others might have been cited here; but *cf.* K. A.

Popper, *The Open Society and Its Enemies* (Routledge & Kegan Paul, London, 1952), and D. Crossman (ed.) *The God That Failed* (Bantam Books; New York, 1952) with contributions by A. Koestler, B. Wright, L. Fischer, I. Silone, A. Gide and S. Spender.

[44] F. Stern, "Der Nationalsozialismus als Versuchung" in *Reflexionen finsterer Zeit* (O. Hofius ed. Mohr/Siebeck, Tübingen, 1984).

[45] F. Neumann, *Behemoth* (Octagon Books, New York, 1963).

[46] Thus in the "remark about the name Behemoth" at the beginning of the book.

[47] Thus at the end of the Third Part in the section entitled "Behemoth."

INDEX